INDOOR PLANTS:
keeping them alive and well

INDOOR PLANTS:
keeping them alive and well

by **Victor Minot** FRHS

W. Foulsham & Co. Ltd.

London · New York · Toronto · Cape Town · Sydney

For
Eve, Val, Vera and Stevie
whose encouragement was appreciated

W Foulsham & Company Limited, Yeovil Road,
Slough, Berkshire SL1 4JH

ISBN 0-572-01013-3
© Copyright. W Foulsham & Co Ltd 1981

Designed by Peter Constable Ltd
Printed in Hong Kong

Contents

Introduction

It's a tough life being a house plant!

By the time the young plants arrive in your home they have already survived many perils. Raised in a large greenhouse or in a nursery, with thousands of others, they have had to adapt to the 'averaged' conditions which enable several types to be housed together.

Individual attention and cosseting have not been their lot, yet they have managed to survive. They have been exposed to draughts and chills when the doors of their great glass house have been opened. There have been regular dowsings with strange and unpleasant chemicals; the fact that these prevent attacks by pests or diseases does not make them any more attractive to the plants than curative medicine to a sick child. However, despite their discomforts, the young plants do survive and thrive.

When they reach saleable size and condition, they are placed in trays—usually 24 pots to a tray—and then in bushel boxes which allow stacking. A bumpy ride through noxious traffic fumes to the Flower Market follows. There, for a time, the plants will remain on shelves in much darker, colder surroundings than the greenhouse that they recently left. The more tender ones will be shielded in thick tubes of newspaper. Others, desperate for humidity, will have polythene bags placed over them. It is crude consideration, but it works; the plants survive and, in time, are transferred from the market to a florist's shop, where it is much darker than it was in the greenhouse, and colder too. The atmosphere is humid, which suits some plants—others are obliged to put up with it, and they do. As the product of millions of years of evolution and adaptation, their species have already survived centuries of climatic changes and the weather's vagaries. They do not succumb easily to adversity; if it is temporary they usually manage to survive.

Not only do the plants survive, they even retain their saleable good looks! Life is tough for them, but then it always has been. As with all living things, their strongest instinct is survival, and they've become rather good at it. Man has eliminated many of the hard knocks which Nature would have imposed, but he has replaced them with others of his own contriving.

Sometimes the florist will put the hardier plants on the pavement outside the shop, where they may suffer sun and traffic heat, dust and fumes from the road, returning later to the cool, moist air inside the shop, which becomes dark and chill as night arrives.

The real troubles begin when one of the plants is bought and taken into a human home as a sort of vegetable pet. The plant is pretty and has cost money, so that it must be cared for, and it usually suffers death by kindness. If a tenth of the well-meaning trouble lavished upon indoor plants was devoted to learning about their nature and their needs, the casualty rate would be halved overnight.

A popular phrase in our technological age is 'When all else fails—read the instructions'. We have become so conditioned to modern marvels that we usually get away with this conduct in our haste to 'see it go'. With plants, however, it does not work! If you leave the instructions on how to tend them until last, then you need not bother—the plants will be dead. You must acquire the information first, and not in a press button fashion. Intelligent thought has to be applied and that is why success is so rewarding. A well-grown plant is an achievement of which you can feel justifiably proud.

Plants are more human than you think!

All life forms on earth had their origins in the same primeval slime, millions of years ago. When organic life developed, different sections of it took varying paths and adapted for survival. If you had been born in sunny, humid Malaya, for example, and had later emigrated to a colder clime you would adapt to it if possible. You would not sit in the hot room of a Turkish bath under television arc lights. Conditions there would certainly be humid and bright, but they would also debilitate you and even kill you. So it is with plants. If you try even partly to approach the conditions that the plant would regard as ideal, it will do its best to meet you halfway. It really does want to live and will try very hard to do so.

To grow indoor plants successfully does not require a professional knowledge of botany. What you do need are green fingers. There is an air of mystique about the tag which those possessed of green fingers foster by basking modestly in the praise of their less gifted friends. It is all a gigantic confidence trick. Green fingers are available almost within minutes to all who care to develop them. You simply have to identify with your plants. If they need a drink, the soil will tell you so by its dryness. Using tepid water to restore it to the correct condition *is* possessing green fingers—but if you merely glance at your watch, decide arbitrarily that it is watering time and drench the poor plant with a pint of icy water, whether it wants it or not, you have probably killed or waterlogged it and it is not your fingers that are green!

Later in this book you will find pictures of indoor plants accompanied by instructions for their care. Instructions create a problem. If you are told vaguely to 'feed occasionally' you will quite rightly wonder what it means. Occasionally during the day, the week or the month? An alternative would be to give a positive instruction like 'feed once weekly'. But that is not necessarily good advice, either. If the climate, real or artificial, is such that it promotes vigorous growth, you will know that from the plant's appearance. If the plant is consuming energy, then it will need food to replace it. During periods when it is less active, and using its food more slowly, the plant will require little or no feeding. Similar reasoning is necessary for watering and all the other necessities of life which you provide.

The one instruction missing from most books is one which should be common to all of them, let's call it Plant-Think. You will discover that it is almost identical to 'thinking about people' or 'caring for them'.

Cerisier Royal.

P. J. Redouté

Where do you expect them to live?

What sort of indoor plant should you buy and how do you make your choice?

Many orchids are a joy to behold, but it is impracticable to keep them as indoor plants because they demand the steamy heat of the jungle. Though you would probably succumb to the atmosphere in time to avoid bankruptcy from the fuel bills, a more practical approach is necessary. The plants you purchase must be able to accept the conditions you can provide, so check what those conditions are. In which positions do you wish to grow plants? Having decided upon that, you need to consider each spot separately and select suitable plants for each one. For example:

The main window

Let us assume that it is broad, the sill is 25 cm (10 in) wide, and the sun reaches it only late in the day. As it is not shaded by nearby buildings, it is very light. It is free from draughts, and there is no radiator below. The room temperature is rarely under 15 °C (60 °F)

This position is fine for many plants. No strong sun; the sill is wide enough to take plant saucers for pots up to 12½ cm (5 in); the temperature is in a good range. Only at night, in winter, when heavy curtains may be drawn, will it be necessary to protect some of the more sensitive plants. You can grow almost anything you like!

The narrower side window

We will assume that this faces east and gets a lot of sunlight. The sill is 25 cm (10 in) wide. There is a radiator beneath it. The only draught is an upward one from the radiator giving the spot a higher than general room temperature.

This window is difficult. Most plants will dislike the conditions; all will dry out quickly and easily. A sturdy cactus would probably manage best to cope with the situation.

The large expanse of wall facing the main window

This gets reasonable light from the window and is never in direct sunlight. It is away from the door and is fairly draught-free. It enjoys room temperature.

The wall is a fine spot for many foliage plants and lovers of slight shade. There is space for a climber or two to be supported and room on the floor to install a small indoor garden. The temperature is good.

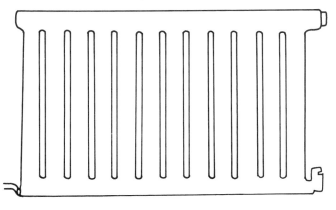

The small alcove beside the door

A shaded, draughty spot where the temperature constantly fluctuates as the door is constantly opened and closed. This is an inhospitable spot; many plants would find the conditions impossible.

Having established the conditions, you can now select plants which are suitable.

The main window. Good conditions. Some sunlight.

Chlorophytum, Cordyline, Ficus decora, Peperomia and *Sansevieria* are all foliage plants which could be used. Most flowering plants too will be happy in this spot, but they are rarely permanent residents. Normally they are moved elsewhere when their display is over. Amongst those suitable are: *Beloperone guttata* (Shrimp plant), *Zonal Pelargonium* (Geranium), *Impatiens sultanii* (Busy Lizzie) and many others.

The side window. This is a hot, inhospitable site.

Try *Coleus* (Flame Nettle), *Beloperone guttata* (Shrimp Plant), *Zonal Pelargonium* (Geranium) or a Cactus. Be sure to provide some humidity.

The wall position. Foliage plants.
Ficus elastica (Rubber Plant), *Monstera deliciosa* (Swiss Cheese Plant), *Maranta* (Prayer Plant), *Adiantum* (Maidenhair Fern), all other foliage plants which accept the room's temperature range. The position will also prove good for many flowering plants, including Gloxinias, *Saintpaulia* (African Violets) and a number of others.

The alcove near the door. A very hostile spot.
The attractive *Cyperus* (Umbrella Plant) will probably survive there. The *Chlorophytum* (Spider Plant) will also possibly withstand it, but may be rather pale. Other plants worth trying are *Zebrina* or *Tradescantia* (Wandering Jew) and *Hedera helix* (Common Ivy).

All we have done here is to examine the positions and identify some suitable plants. How to keep those plants alive and well will be discussed in succeeding chapters.

What's your type?

Foliage plants

The majority will be permanent residents, and as long as the right conditions are provided they will remain elegant and attractive during the entire year. They will repay correct care, for without it they can become unsightly and cease to be an asset to the room they are intended to decorate.

Foliage plants which flower
If kept alive and well, these will be permanent

occupants of the room and may be expected to flower there. Their leaves will last throughout the year and are often just as attractive as those of the foliage plants.

Cacti and succulents

Also permanent residents; some will even flower in room conditions, provided that their needs are met. They will survive quite happily at 5–10 C (40–50 F) but they cannot stand frost.

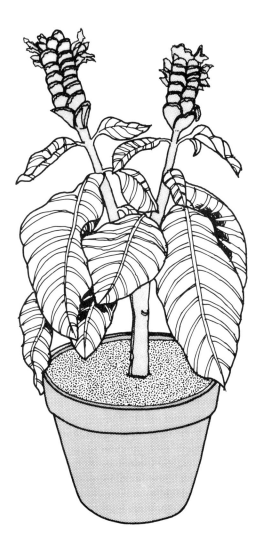

Flowering indoor plants

There are vast numbers of them. Generally, they flower abundantly and will remain in bloom for a long time in room conditions. Members of this group are available for almost every period of the year and, in winter especially, those available can be the source of considerable visual pleasure. Normally they are discarded when flowering has ceased, although some varieties may be kept if a greenhouse is available.

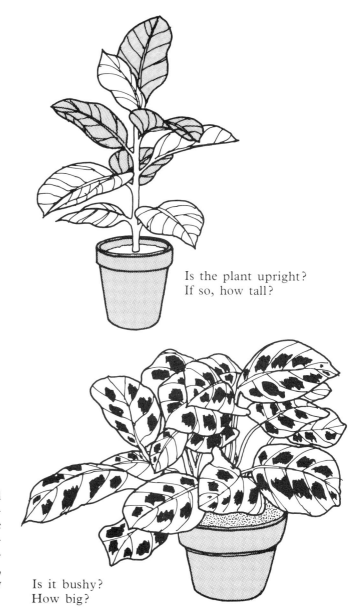

Is the plant upright?
If so, how tall?

Now that the basic groups have been defined it is important to understand the individual characteristics possessed by single members of any of the groups. This information is vital—without it your indoor garden could lack form or style. Good combination of plants is an art form akin to flower arranging, and to achieve it you need to know each plant's way of growing, or habit.

Is it bushy?
How big?

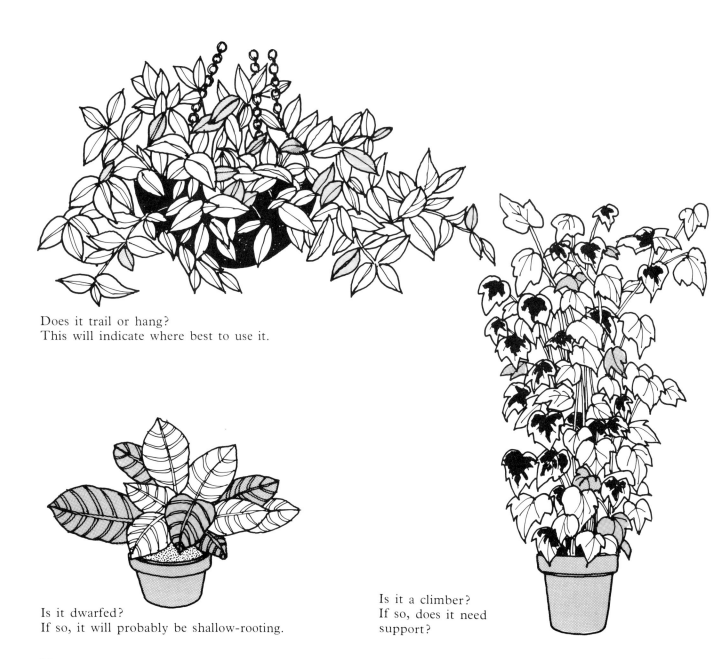

Does it trail or hang?
This will indicate where best to use it.

Is it dwarfed?
If so, it will probably be shallow-rooting.

Is it a climber?
If so, does it need support?

Is it slow growing?
If so, it may be placed
almost anywhere.

Is it vigorous?
It could grow too fast for some uses.

Clearly, problems would follow the planting of the vigorous Kangaroo Vine *(Cissus antartica)*—which would quickly furnish a room divider—in a small indoor garden; a dwarf Ivy would be much more suitable.

Let there be light

In a sense, light to a plant equals food! Human beings live on chemical substances, but are unable to survive on them until they have been rendered into absorbable form. The steak you eat, for example, is broken down by the process of digestion.

In the case of plants, chemicals pass into the roots and are conveyed to the leaves through the sap of the plant. But mostly, the plant makes its own food by the process known as photosynthesis; it uses the energy in light—usually sunlight—to make carbohydrates like glucose, sugar and starch from water absorbed through the roots and carbon dioxide from the air. They are enabled to do so by the green chlorophyll in their leaves, which works as a catalyst. Without light no food is built up. If the leaves turn yellow, it means that no food is being manufactured to keep the plant alive.

A photographer's light meter taken outside on a bright day will indicate high intensity; carry it at once into a bright room and the needle will barely register any light at all. Your plant, which once lived in the open, is similarly affected. The lower light level means that less food is made, and the giant of the rain forest grows as a dainty but healthy dwarf.

It is of course true that in nature many plants live in shaded conditions, but even so the total light from all sides considerably exceeds that available from the limited window area of a room. The plants are indoor plants because of their ability to adapt to these low light levels. It is wise to give them all the light that you can make available.

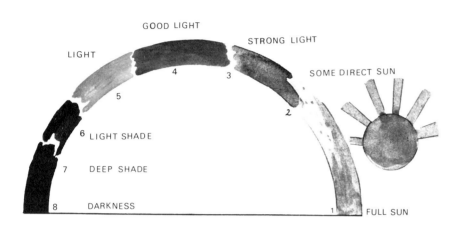

GOOD LIGHT
LIGHT
STRONG LIGHT
SOME DIRECT SUN
4
3
5
2
6 LIGHT SHADE
7 DEEP SHADE
8 DARKNESS
1 FULL SUN

low   high

midday outside on
a bright sunny day

*A floor plan view of
light intensity
produced by 2 windows
in a room 4 x 5 meters*

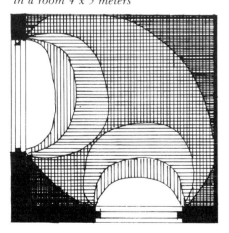

*A cross section view of
the light intensity from
one window*

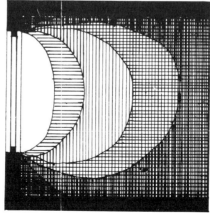

low   high

same time and day in
a room with a large
window and excellent light

 *90-100%
ideal*

*70-90%
very good*

*50-70%
good*

*30-50%
medium*

 *10-30%
bad*

 *—10%
growth ceases*

Warmth—keep it constant

Few indoor plants require, or will even tolerate, more than 22 °C (70 °F) of warmth, yet in their tropical homes they are happy with much higher temperatures. This is because there is a balance between the *light* and the *warmth*.

In nature, warmth and light come from the sun. At the time when it is at its brightest it also gives most heat. If, by some means, its light is reduced (say, by the shade of trees) the temperature then goes down.

Your indoor plant is receiving comparatively little light and therefore needs less warmth to maintain a suitable balance. It has already been shown that less food is made in the leaves when the level of light is reduced. At the same time they will be giving off less moisture. Too high a temperature in relation to the light will result in excessive evaporation and the leaves will dry out.

What plants do object to are sudden sharp fluctuations in temperature. Imagine the effect of a cool bright winter's day with good light and a little heat. At nightfall, even with artificial illumination, the light is reduced to a fraction of its daytime level. The heating is increased, however, to keep the humans warm, and the temperature rises considerably. Each in itself is bad enough, but the change in the light-warmth balance is of gigantic proportions.

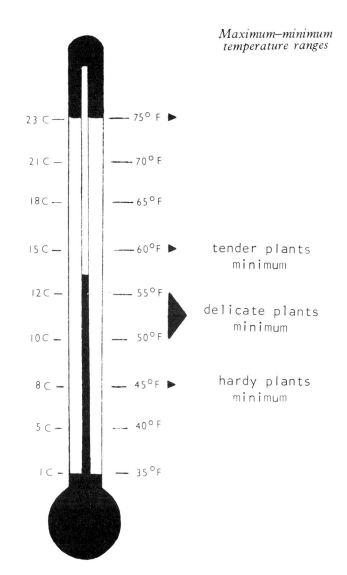

Maximum–minimum temperature ranges

23 C	75° F ▶
21 C	70° F
18 C	65° F
15 C	60° F ▶ tender plants minimum
12 C	55° F ▶ delicate plants minimum
10 C	50° F
8 C	45° F ▶ hardy plants minimum
5 C	40° F
1 C	35° F

Air—let it circulate

Dust—the enemy

Humans need fresh air; their lungs extract oxygen from it and they exhale the carbon dioxide. Unless the air is changed regularly, the oxygen in it is exhausted.

Plants have roughly similar needs and the air around them should circulate freely to help remove traces of gas or other toxic fumes. Good ventilation also has a mild prophylactic effect. Plants given a regular supply of fresh air, provided it is not accompanied by a sharp drop in temperature, are less likely to be attacked by mildew or fungus diseases.

Ventilation and fresh air emphatically do not mean draughts, which cause sharp drops in temperature and humidity—very harmful to all indoor plants, even the most sturdy.

Dust is a plant enemy which makes the foliage look dull, blocks leaf pores and inhibits the plant's respiration. In towns, it often contains damaging or corrosive chemicals. A covering of dust also reduces the life-giving light which the leaf needs.

Dust can be removed by spraying and gently sponging the leaves with clean water. Ignore very young leaves until they grow larger so as to avoid damaging them. If the foliage is extremely dusty, it should be gently brushed with a feather duster before washing; otherwise the plant pores will be clogged with a sticky mud containing the unwanted chemicals and, after drying out, the plant will be worse off than it was before it was treated.

It is possible to polish large strong leaves with specially developed cleaners such as 'Bio Leaf Shine'. Apply by gently wiping the leaves with a pad of cotton wool soaked in the liquid. The shine is usually long lasting and does help to keep the leaves dust-free.

Water—don't drown it

Water is essential to plants, they cannot live without it. With few exceptions they cannot live *in* it either! More plants die from drowning than any other cause. This most commonly occurs when people stick to rigid rules about watering and at, say 9.0 am give each plant its daily half pint, whether it wants it or not.

Plants with thick, fleshy leaves hold more water and need less frequent watering than thinner leaved varieties. Thinner leaves have much greater surface areas, their evaporation loss is higher, and the plants need more regular attention. Another important factor is the season. In winter, growth slows and may even stop. The plant is less active and the demand for water is reduced. The situation is reversed when growth begins again. As growth becomes more vigorous, more water is required. As temperature and light are increased, so growth is stimulated, and the plants again need more water.

It should be clear that the nearest a plant can get to being a regular 'Daily Pinta' drinker is to be a water lily. Having decided the factors which govern the demand for water, it is now necessary to say something about the type of water. There are, in fact, a number of kinds, but we are concerned with two— tap water and soft rainwater.

Rainwater (chemically neutral) is virtually pure. Even when collected in a butt from the roof it will contain only odd impurities that are unlikely to adversely affect the plant. It is usually warmer than tap water. Its lime content is either zero or insignificant. You can easily 'go wrong' with tap water, never with rainwater.

Tap water (normally alkaline) always contains chemicals; chlorine, for example, is used to purify it. Considerable quantities of calcium (lime) are frequently present because tap water is collected in reservoirs from watersheds, which in many places are of limestone. Nowadays, fluoride is often added, too.

Lime is not a plant food; its function is to interact with other material in the soil. By doing so it sets free nutrients which would not otherwise be soluble, and makes them available to the plant roots. This suits a large group of plants which accept the alkalinity of the soil created by the lime. Such plants are known as 'lime tolerant'.

However, almost all indoor plants prefer an acid soil which must therefore be lime-free. The constant use of tap water containing lime results in a build-up of lime in the soil and makes it inhospitable to indoor plants. Such plants will respond by turning yellow, looking sick and finally dying.

When rainwater is not available, the answer is to boil tap water and then leave it to cool before using it on your indoor plants. Most of the lime content will be deposited in the kettle in the form of fur.

For those interested in technical terms, the alkaline-acid conditions of compost, etc., are regularly referred to as the pH Factor, and the following is given as a guide.

pH $6\frac{1}{2}$	Slightly acid
pH 7	Neutral
pH $7\frac{1}{2}$	Slightly alkaline

Watering is the key

No area of indoor plant care demands the ability to 'plant-think' more than the question of when to water. *Never* go by the clock, but think in terms of maintaining *the right soil condition*. Each day, take whatever action is necessary to provide the right amount of water for each individual plant. The right soil condition for each plant is described under their individual entry.

To give water when the plants need it means that you must regularly test the soil first by pressing your thumb on its surface.

Wet Soil feels soggy and lifeless; the thumb makes a mark which tends to linger and particles of soil will adhere to the thumb.

Moist Soil will feel springy and the thumb mark will probably disappear as it would if you pressed a sponge. Particles of soil will adhere to the thumb.

Dry Soil feels dry and firm, often hard. It will not give to thumb pressure and few, if any, particles will adhere to your thumb.

The Watering Technique

First check the soil and decide whether to water!

For watering, use a can of comfortable size with a long, narrow spout which will slip easily under the leaves of the plant and reach the soil at the base of the stems. Fill the space between the soil and the rim of the pot. The water will drain through the soil into the saucer in which the pot is standing. Empty it; do *not* leave this residue in the saucer.

Only two popular indoor plants like the water to be left in the saucer, they are *Cyperus* (Umbrella Plant) and *Helxine* (Mind Your Own Business).

Some plants dislike water in their crowns or on their corms—Gloxinia and Cyclamen are typical examples. It is better to water them from below. To do this, immerse the pots in water to soil level; leave them to soak until the top of the soil feels moist to thumb pressure. This can usually be seen as well—the soil glistens slightly. When they reach this stage, stand the pots somewhere to drain out, and then return them to their growing positions.

If top watering is unavoidable, do so with great care and do not wet the crowns of the plants.

Watering Difficulties

(1) Water runs straight through because soil has dried out and shrunk: remedy this by immersing the pot in bucket or trough with water to soil level. Leave to soak until soil surface glistens. Gently loosen surface soil with an old table fork.

(2) Water not soaking into the soil but remaining on top in a pool: the remedy for this is to prick the surface of the soil with a fork so that it is friable and broken up and then immerse the pot in water as directed in (1) above.

water forms pool on top of pot

water runs through pot

Good Watering

The water permeates the soil, any excess draining into the plant saucer to be emptied away.

If you are in any doubt as to whether your plant needs water or not—wait another day. Remember, more plants die from over-watering than any other reason.

In winter, in unheated or cool rooms, water in the morning. *Don't* use cold water, make sure it is tepid or lukewarm.

In summer, never water if the plant is in full sunlight. If you do, and the leaves are splashed, the droplets can act like tiny lenses and burn the leaves.

good watering

plant saucer

Humidity is important too

To most house plants, moist air is more vital than warm air; they have a desperate need for humidity. Many of them had their origins in the rain forests or other lush growing areas of the world, where good supplies of light, warmth and food led to vigorous growth. This, in turn, resulted in larger leaves or many smaller ones increasing the total leaf areas in order to keep pace with the requirements of food to sustain growth.

These environments were made lush by plentiful rainfall. The vigorous growth would soon have run into an evaporation problem but for the high rainfall. Although high temperatures cause evaporation of moisture from the soil, moist warm air is retained near the ground by the tree canopy overhead—hence 'steaming jungle'.

Our indoor plants are often scaled-down models of these jungle plants, and their humidity needs are scaled down too, as is their light-warmth-water balance. But they have evolved with humidity as a vital factor of the life balance and must have it in similar proportions to the other factors in the balance.

There are some indoor plants which do not need humidity. Cacti are the obvious example, originating as they do from the arid areas of the world. The need for survival has obliged them to find means of countering the hostile conditions forced upon them by climatic changes. They developed thick, water-retaining combined leaves and stems. In many cases they grew round or oval to present the smallest surface area possible. A sphere contains the maximum volume in the minimum surface area and cacti have learned to minimise evaporation by conforming to this shape as closely as they can. They grab all the water they can obtain and give off as little as possible.

Creating humidity

Central heating can be a boon to the indoor plant enthusiast since it ensures good control over temperature. Regrettably, central heating also dries the air in the room so that some means of providing humidity for the plants must be found. Since it is both impractical and undesirable to increase the humidity of the whole room to the degree required, a Mini-Climate must be created in the air surrounding the plants. This can be achieved fairly easily.

1. Moist Air Bath

Half fill a large plant saucer with pebbles. Push into them a smaller saucer in an inverted position to give the pot steady support. Add water to a level slightly below the base of the plant pot. Replace evaporation loss as necessary.

2. Moist Air Bath

For plants in a trough or stand

Fill space between container and the pot with peat. Keep this peat packing thoroughly moist at all times.

3. The Steam Bath

Place a brick, or block of wood, in a large basin and pour in enough boiling water to reach just below the level of the top of the brick. Stand

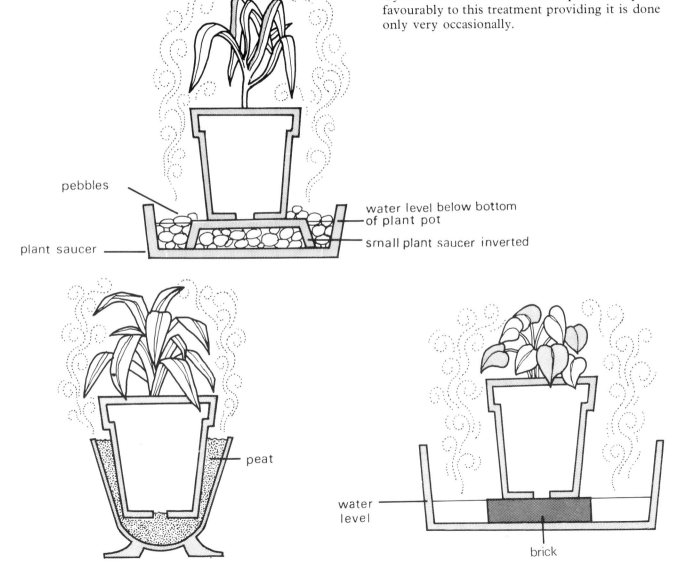

the flower pot on the brick for five minutes. Cyclamen and some other plants respond favourably to this treatment providing it is done only very occasionally.

pebbles

plant saucer

water level below bottom of plant pot

small plant saucer inverted

peat

water level

brick

Spraying

Give it a rest

Indoors this is best done with a hand sprayer that produces a very fine spray, almost a mist, which will prevent any droplets from collecting on leaves and damaging them. It should be done in the morning so that the plants will be dry by nightfall.

A small pump-up (pneumatic) pressure spray does the job very well. The fine spray can easily be directed under the foliage as well as over the top. It is also possible with one of these to spray *in situ* such plants as *Monstera*, etc., without soaking the walls. The same type of pressure spray may also be used for pesticides.

A small hand-operated pneumatic pressure spray

To provide lucid comparisons in this book, where possible the plants have been likened to people. Dealing with the rest period of plants in this way, however, places a slight strain on the analogy which is intended to provide a mental image rather than to be regarded as scientific fact.

Normally people take two kinds of rest period. A daily one which we call sleep, and a seasonal one, usually in the summer, which we know as our annual holiday. In many ways, but with some exceptions, plants parallel these rest periods, though their annual holiday will usually be timed to meet grey wintery skies.

During sleep our metabolic rate eases, our breathing slows and we neither eat nor drink. At night the light which the leaves use in converting nutrients into plant food is largely absent. The leaves demand less nutrition from the roots which reduce the rate at which they absorb the soil solution containing the nutrients. The metabolic rate of the plant has slowed down. Some plants close their leaves or fold their leaves during the daily rest period. This prevents chilling from evaporation. Bedclothes could be said to have a similar effect.

Different plants utilize their seasonal rest period in different ways but some parallels still exist. During our annual holiday we do eat and drink. We also relax and slow down. The adrenal glands are given less exercise and our 'batteries are re-charged'.

Many house plants are evergreen; during their rest period they behave in a way comparable to

people. Growth slows substantially, allowing the plant to 'take it easy'. Reduced growth results in a lessened demand for nutrients from the soil solution, less light is needed for the making of plant food, and less water is needed to provide adequate soil solution.

Dull winter skies usually result in a reduction in light so inhibiting growth. The roots reduce their intake of soil solution. If at this time excessive water is given the roots will not absorb it and it will lie around them, causing them to drown or rot.

Deciduous plants which shed their leaves become dormant for a period and can be likened to a hibernating animal. The animal's metabolic rate reduces, its breathing slows and it neither eats nor drinks. Its energy consumption is minimal. If you filled its hibernation burrow with food and water it would suffocate or drown.

Your deciduous house plant will react in a similar way. It is not consuming energy nor food or water because growth is suspended. All that it needs are rest, a modicum of humidity and a life sustaining temperature. If you feed and water it during its rest period its roots will suffocate or drown.

The rest periods of different plants varies and information about these periods will be found elsewhere in the text. A shortened or prolonged rest period will not result in 'Making it Spectacular', but it is unlikely to be lethal. To attempt to keep the plant 'going' when it wants to rest almost certainly will be lethal! Again we are brought back to 'Plant-Think'. Imagine the result of having food pushed into your mouth whilst in a deep sleep. Think of the effect of being forced to sustain 'Rat-race' pace whilst on holiday.

If you can feed and water your plants before mid-day, and if you allow them a seasonal rest when they need it, you are well on the way to 'Making them Spectacular'.

Feeding your indoor plants

During the course of centuries, your indoor plant evolved and adapted in a natural environment. The rain watered it, light and warmth were provided by the sun, and the earth itself held the chemicals used by the plant to make food. Even if the plant died, or was killed, its constituents returned to the soil to become food for its successor. When supplies close at hand ran low, rain would probably leach more chemicals through the soil to the plant. Failing this, the roots would spread and forage further afield.

Compare with this the artificial environment in which we expect indoor plants to flourish. There is no rain to wash the leaves, or to dissolve the soil chemicals; instead we spray and water. As the roots are confined inside pots, they cannot spread to seek more nourishment. When the plants have consumed the nutrients in the compost we give them, we have to provide fresh supplies of synthetic food which match their synthetic climate and environment. Incredibly, in these conditions, with the simple addition of what we call Plant-Think they thrive, growing strong and beautiful.

To produce healthy growth, fine flowers and good foliage, plants must have supplies of nitrogen, phosphorus, potassium (potash) and numerous trace elements. They are best provided in a compound fertilizer that contains them all. Complete fertilizers may be easily obtained either in solid or in liquid form, chemical or organic. The liquid is by far the best for indoor plants. 'Baby Bio' is just one example of the good proprietary brands. It is a highly concentrated plant food which contains extracts of humus and seaweed, vital organic elements necessary to plant health. Simply diluted with water, it gives an even distribution of nutrients to the plant roots throughout the pot, avoiding the danger of starving the roots in one section of the pot while giving those in another a concentration so strong that it is toxic.

Always remember to feed plants sparingly; tiny, balanced doses are what is required. If a plant needs more nourishment, it will show symptoms which you can easily and quickly rectify. The effects of over-feeding are much more harmful. Some plants will use more of one chemical than another. In that case, a build-up of surplus nutrients in the compost may result in a concentration that is harmful to the plant. Moderation in the supply of feed should avoid this calamity, but if it occurs, feeding must be stopped. Watering with rainwater, which can dissolve more chemicals than tap water, may help to remove the surplus. Nevertheless, the plant will have suffered a serious check. It may take a considerable time to recover and will, perhaps, lose its verve for life, always remaining rather a sickly specimen. To repeat the message then: if in doubt, don't!

Two vital rules that must be observed when feeding indoor plants:
1. Never feed a 'dry' plant—get the soil into the right condition first.
2. Never, never, never give an extra 'slurp' of food as though it were a treat—it could easily prove fatal!

Foliar feeds, specially formulated nutrients for spraying on the leaves, can be another aid in keeping your plants healthy. Like the systemic insecticides and fungicides, they are absorbed by the plant. They promote healthy, good-looking leaves and thus supplement normal feeding, but they do not provide an alternative to it. They act very rapidly.

You will find it very helpful to understand the prime function of the main constituents of a good plant food: so do read this.

Nitrogen

In a natural environment, nitrogen is obtained from nitrates in the humus contained in rich soil. It is necessary for growth and the production of good foliage with rich green colour; an excess will result in lush, soft growth and fewer flowers.

Phosphorus

Obtained from phosphates in the soil, phosphorus is essential for the formation of strong, healthy root systems resulting in vigorous plants which produce good flowers and seeds. Plants lacking the chemical will be stunted, with poorly developed root systems which, in extreme cases, cannot adequately support the plant.

Potassium

Potash has been called 'chemical sunshine' because of its effect. It assists the production of good flowers and fruit. An inadequate supply results in small flowers of poor colour; stems are brittle, and the plants are prone through weakness to attack from disease.

For answers to the questions of when to feed, and how much, we are back to Plant-Think. It is obvious that a tiny, slow-growing cactus will need far less food than a large and vigorous Rubber Plant. During the entire spring and summer, the cactus will be happy with about three feeds while the Rubber Plant will need feeding at almost every watering.

The system to adopt is to water those plants not in need of feeding. When they have been dealt with, refill the watering can, add the liquid plant food and water the remainder. They are then fed and watered simultaneously. The quantities given should be those advised by the makers of the food used.

What did I do wrong?

Plants die for several reasons—

1. Drying out

Failure to provide in sufficient quantities the water on which life depends will cause leaves to wilt and, eventually, they turn brown and shrivel up. In time the plants will die.

2. Over-watering

This is the greatest plant-killer of all. In winter its effects are rapid. When the roots are drowning they lose efficiency; the leaves droop, and the plant appears to be short of water. If more water is given, however, the plant will soon be dead.

The following signs will help you to tell whether wilting is caused by too much moisture or too little:

a. Thumb pressure on the surface will show if the soil is dry or wet;
b. Dry wilt usually shows browning and shrivelling of leaves;
c. Wet wilt usually causes the leaves to turn yellow and become floppy and limp.

3. Draughts

It is not so much the passage of air which is damaging as the sudden drop in temperature and humidity that accompanies the draught. In nature, plants can withstand wind because it never affects warmth and humidity to the same degree as a draught in a room.

4. Chilly nights

Most plants will stand lower temperatures than is commonly believed, but they cannot endure large changes in temperature.

Take, for example, a plant that spends the day enjoying winter sunshine on the window sill of a heated room. When curtains are drawn at night, the plant is in what can become a frost pocket. It is insulated by the curtains from the warmth that remains in the room and cold from outside penetrates the window glass resulting in icy conditions.

The obvious remedy is to bring plants into the warmest part of the room on cold nights. Tender stems can be given the added protection of several thicknesses of newspaper wrapped around pot and plant.

5. Lack of humidity

The dry atmosphere caused by modern central heating often results in shrivelled leaves and, ultimately, the death of the plant—methods of combating these adverse conditions have already been described.

Give some thought to where you place your plants. Do not put them on the mantelpiece over an open fire, or over a radiator, unless there is a means of deflecting rising heat.

6. Hot sunshine

Geraniums and a few other indoor plants will not object to full sunlight provided that the pot and soil are not exposed. Most other plants will dry out, suffering scorched leaves and flowers.

7. Lack of light

Continual deep shade will kill almost all plants.

8. Fumes

The fumes given off by gas, coal fires and oil heaters can be toxic in varying degrees. Careful ventilation is the only possible remedy.

When they look sick

1. Pale spindly growth
In winter this can be the result of the plants being kept too moist or too warm for the light available. The balance is wrong. During growth periods it can be caused by lack of light or by starvation which can be overcome by feeding.

2. Yellowing leaves which drop
This can be caused by draughts, lack of humidity or over-watering.

3. Dry brown leaf tips or margins
Sunburn (scorching), water splashes on leaves; lack of humidity, fumes, over-watering or over-feeding can all cause these symptoms.

4. Dropping flower buds
A change in the position of the plant to one it finds less acceptable; over-watering; lack of humidity, sometimes over-feeding just as the buds are forming.

5. Rotting leaves or stem
This is caused by fungus attack, over-watering in winter, open wounds or water splashes on the leaves.

6. Wilt
The plant may be waterlogged, too dry or too hot and dry.

7. Yellow leaves
If they are otherwise healthy then the cause is either an accumulation of lime in the soil or some soil deficiency.

8. Sudden and considerable leaf shedding
Dry roots, large changes in temperature or light levels, fumes and draughts can all be the cause.

9. Poor contrast in colour in variegated foliage
The reason for this is always insufficient light.

10. Poor performance in growth season
It may need re-potting or feeding, or it may be over-watered.

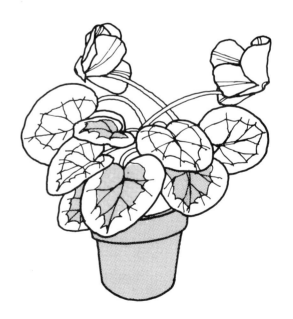

Preventive medicine

Human beings usually thrive in a healthy environment simply because their living conditions are good. They do not suffer such misfortunes as exposure or undernourishment. Even so, they are not immune to attack from viruses and similar enemies. In most cases, the effects are curable, and in many instances prevention is possible.

Your indoor plants are in a similar situation. By now, you know how to maintain the conditions they need to keep them alive and well. A healthy environment is the greatest protection they can have, but they are still vulnerable to attack from insects and fungus. To notice that the shoots of your favourite plant look pale and distorted and immediately act on the assumption that it needs feeding will achieve nothing if the cause is aphids beneath the leaves. There is only one method of identifying attack by pests, and that is to know what the different pests look like and examine the plants regularly for signs of any attack. ·

Fortunately, there are proprietary products to cover any eventuality. In the main, they are simple, safe and clean to use; many of them are in aerosol form. Each of the remedies produced by a reputable company carries clear, precise instructions for use and, since you are handling potent chemicals, you must follow them carefully. An overdose will have serious effects on the plant.

Fertilizers, pesticides and fungicides are widely available from Garden Centres and Nurseries. To get rid of sap suckers like greenfly, spray the pests with

Systemic insecticides function from within the plant system

insecticide. Look, too, for systemic insecticides and fungicides which act through the plant's own system and are comparable to immunization in animals. Systemics are sprayed on the plant which then absorbs them. In the case of such an insecticide, the plant becomes poisonous to its attackers—one bite into the plant and the insect dies. With systemic fungicides also, the plant becomes a hostile host, and the fungal attack fails. Some can even be applied after the disease has taken hold; they still have a curative effect, but it is better to spray beforehand and prevent infection. Systemics are valuable aids; they protect the plant against a hidden insect or patch of mildew that you might otherwise overlook. The application has to be repeated at intervals as the systemic effect diminishes and new growth should also be sprayed.

Although pests attack indoor plants far less frequently than plants growing in the open, the comfortable conditions and the absence of predators result in a fairly quick growth in the severity of an attack when it occurs. Early discovery and treatment are very important. Six insect pests are listed which may attack your indoor plants. Others exist, but it is unlikely that your plants will be affected by them.

Diseases

To guard against pests and diseases, do not use unsterilized garden soil indoors. Microbes which cause root and stem rot, together with insects which attack roots, are to be found in it. Soil can be cleaned by hanging in a cotton bag over boiling water in a closed container. It is much simpler, however, to buy sterilized compost from your nurseryman. 'Baby Bio' Potting Compost for example is reliable, widely available and not very expensive, or there are many other proprietary brands.

As well as insect pests, there are many plant diseases, but fortunately comparatively few of them affect those growing indoors. The two which you should guard against are:

1. Rot
This is usually associated with over-watering, especially in winter. Root-rot will result in the loss of the plant.

To control it
Always use sterilized soil, never unsterilized soil. Keep plant warm and don't over-water, especially in winter. Spray with 'Benlate' or similar proprietary fungicide.

2. Mildew (Botrytis)
White or grey mould on stems and leaves of plants. More frequent in Summer, and often the result of a stagnant humid atmosphere in which the spores of the disease thrive.

To control it

Improve growing conditions and ensure good ventilation. Spray with 'Benlate' or other proprietary fungicide.

Preventative action

When it is necessary to remove a leaf, stem or flower which will leave a moist open wound, spray the cut gently with flowers of sulphur (obtainable from any chemist). This is an old, proven remedy which will inhibit fungal disease from becoming established in the wound.

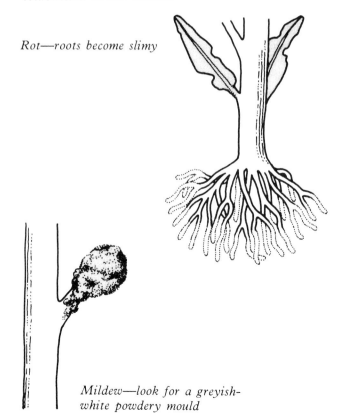

Rot—roots become slimy

Mildew—look for a greyish-white powdery mould

Pests

Blackfly, Greenfly

Breed in numerous groups on new shoots and under leaves, which become distorted and the plant is weakened. Some leaves may fall and the affected parts of the plant are covered with sticky honey dew exuded by the insects. The presence of ants always invites closer investigation. They farm aphids in much the same way as a dairy farmer does cows, in order to harvest the honey dew, and will transfer the aphids to other plants to breed new 'herds'.

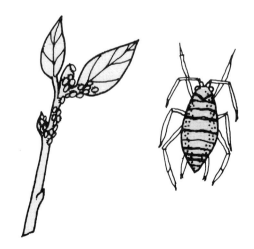

To control

Spray with 'Bio Sprayday' or other proprietary brand of greenfly killer at the first sign of attack.

Red Spider Mites

Minute pests which attack the undersides of leaves, on which a white webbing is sometimes visible. The upper surface of the leaves becomes dry and brittle, and the plant is weakened. These insects multiply rapidly and often remain unseen until large groups are present. A magnifying glass aids early discovery; try a straight clear glass filled with water. Through it you should see the culprit even though its image will be distorted. They like hot dry conditions and are very persistent.

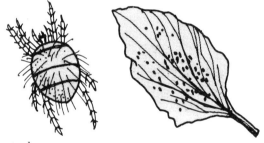

To control

Spray with liquid derris and repeat at an interval of two days.

White Flies

Tiny moth-like flies which suck sap. Foliage becomes mottled and growth is weakened. Infested areas become covered in sticky honey dew.

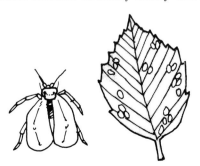

To control

Spray with 'Bio Sprayday' or other proprietary brand of greenfly killer. Repeat after three days.

Scale Insects

Small immobile waxy shells found clinging to stems and leaves of shrubby indoor plants. Growth is weakened and sticky honey dew is exuded over the plant.

To control

Use a matchstick tipped with cotton wool soaked in methylated spirit to rub the pests from the plant.

Thrips

Tiny, black, winged insects which attack leaves and flowers, leaving white dots and streaks. Growth of plant is stunted.

This is a fairly uncommon pest.

To control

Spray with Malathion or Topgard dust.

Mealy Bugs

Small pests with a white, cottony covering; found on the undersides of leaves and on the joints of stems during summer.

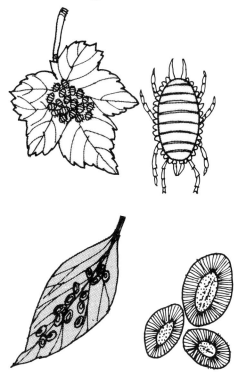

To control

Use a matchstick tipped with cotton wool soaked in methylated spirits to dab pests off plants.

Pots for your indoor plants

When you have acquired skill at keeping your indoor plants alive and well, they will thrive and increase in size. Inevitably you will have to transfer them into larger pots. When you come to do this, make sure you select the right pot. They come in a variety of sizes and can be made of clay or plastic in the standard or deep-rimmed shapes.

The clay pot

This is frequently cheaper to buy. The advantage of a clay pot is that, because it is porous, waterlogging is a little less likely to happen. The clay pot often has a poor shape, however, and may stand badly. It also breaks very easily.

The plastic pot

This is much lighter, and is unlikely to break if it is accidentally dropped. The soil temperature is kept more even and less water is needed because the pot is non-porous. It will stand firmly and have a more attractive appearance. Plastic pots can be obtained in decorative shades. A further advantage, especially of the deep-rimmed type, is that these pots stack well without jamming.

Plant saucers

These may be in clay or plastic to match the pots. Not only do they make the pot look more attractive, but they also catch any drainage from the soil inside the pot.

Table of pot sizes

Top diameter of pot		Depth of pot		Distance of soil level from top of pot		Suitable saucer size	
ins	cms	ins	cms	ins	cms	ins	cms
$2\frac{1}{2}$	6	$2\frac{1}{2}$	6	$\frac{3}{8}$	1	4	6
3	9	$3\frac{1}{2}$	12	$\frac{1}{4}$	1	5	10
$4\frac{1}{2}$	12	5	15	$\frac{1}{2}$	1	$6\frac{1}{2}$	14
6	15	6	15	$\frac{3}{4}$	2	9	20
$8\frac{1}{2}$	20	8	20	1	3	10	25
$9\frac{1}{2}$	25	9	25	$1\frac{1}{4}$	3	10	35
12	30	11	27	$1\frac{1}{2}$	4	14	40
15	50	13	35	2	5	18	60

If you decide to use deep-rimmed pots, which are recommended, then the correct soil level is indicated by the bottom of the deep top rim.

Compost for your indoor plants

Having selected a new pot for your indoor plant, be sure to use the right soil to fill it. As suitable loam is not easy to obtain and its quality may be extremely variable, use one of the commercial composts which do not contain loam. These soil-less composts are based on peat and have a great many advantages when compared with their soil-based counterparts.

1. They are easily obtained in bags of varying sizes.
2. They are already sterilized when you buy them, so are ready to use.
3. They are lighter and cleaner to handle.
4. Their quality is consistent.
5. Special types are available to suit plants with special requirements, e.g. lime-free for Azaleas. They can also be obtained with varying fertilizer content.

Proprietary composts will generally contain sufficient constituents to provide normal plant nutrients for a period of eight weeks and feeding is not necessary, or even desirable, during that period. For a few plants, the period may vary slightly, so you should always follow the manufacturers' recommendations.

The composts are normally bought packed in polythene bags, and usually in a rather dry condition. Most of the peat composts are rather difficult to wet although some, such as 'Baby Bio' composts, do contain a wetting agent to make it easier. If possible, open the bag, roll back the top, prick for drainage and leave it out of doors until a downpour of rain does the work for you. Otherwise, smaller amounts must be dampened in a bowl before the compost is used for planting.

When you come to fill your pots, it is important that the material shall not be rammed down too firmly. Excessive pressure compacts the mixture, making impossible the efficient aeration which is vital to the fibrous plant roots. Compacting is also a first step to early waterlogging.

When you buy your compost, also obtain some crushed charcoal. Mix in some of this—enough pieces to cover a dessertspoon for a five inch pot— and it will keep the compost sweet by absorbing some of the toxic chemicals which may build up. Vary the amount of charcoal according to the size of the pot, using this example as a guide.

For indoor plants, well known proprietary brands of soil-less composts are recommended without reservation but for growers who wish to use the internationally famous John Innes composts the different mixtures are listed below.

The John Innes Composts

The Basic Mixture.

7 parts (by bulk) of damp sterilized loam obtained from turves stacked grass-downward until well rotted;

3 parts (by bulk) of damp garden peat;

2 parts (by bulk) of coarse sand;

thoroughly mixed.

John Innes Potting Compost No. 1

For filling pots less than 10 cm (4 ins) in diameter.

To each bushel (30 kg) of the basic mix, add 25 gm ($\frac{3}{4}$ oz) of ground chalk (blackboard chalk, whiting or ground limestone will do).

John Innes Potting Compost No. 2

For filling pots 10 cm (4 ins) to 20 cm (8 ins) diameter.

To each bushel of the basic mix, add 50 gm ($1\frac{3}{4}$ oz) of ground chalk.

John Innes Potting Compost No. 3

For filling pots of over 20 cm ($8\frac{1}{2}$ ins) diameter.

To each bushel of the basic mix, add 70 gm. ($2\frac{1}{2}$ oz) of ground chalk.

For most pot plants use $\frac{2}{3}$ JOHN INNES POTTING COMPOST plus $\frac{1}{3}$ Garden Peat.

For lime-hating plants (Azalea, Begonia, African Violet, Cyclamen and Erica) use the same mixture but omit chalk from the John Innes Potting Compost.

When does it need re-potting?

Many indoor plants thrive happily in pots which look too small for them. In fact, the plant development you are anxious to achieve may actually be frustrated if you transfer the plant to a bigger pot before it is needed. No indoor plant should ever be given a larger container until it is positively potbound. This could be as long as one or two years after purchase, and never in the case of some specimens. Bromeliads, for example, seldom, if ever, become potbound.

The best time to check if your plant needs re-potting is in late spring. Symptoms to look for are:

1. Leaves and stems grow very slowly. Regular feeding in spring and summer fail to achieve any improvement.
2. Compost dries out very quickly and watering is frequently necessary.
3. Plant roots hang from the drainage hole of the pot.

If any of these characteristics are observed a further check should then be made. Allow the plant compost to become slightly dry, so that it does not fall away from the roots as you remove it from the pot. Spread the fingers of one hand across the top of the pot and turn the pot upside down. Gently tap its rim on the edge of a bench, lifting the pot away with the other hand as you do so. The plant with its soil ball adhering will remain in one hand, the pot in the other.

If the plant is potbound, little soil will be

The roots will have pushed through the bottom of the pot

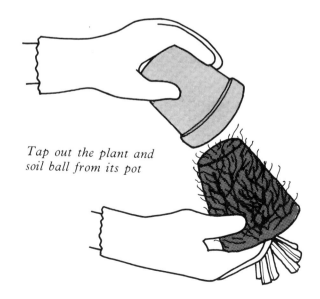

Tap out the plant and soil ball from its pot

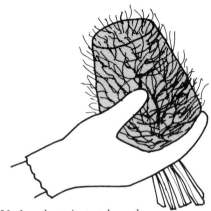

If the plant is pot bound, little soil will be visible

If it is not pot bound replace the pot over soil ball

visible; a tangled mass of roots will wind around the outside of the soil where they have followed the confines of the pot.

It may be that the plant is not potbound, in which case all you have to do is replace the pot over the soil ball and return the whole to an upright position; no harm will have been done.

If you find that the plant needs re-potting, check that the new pot you have selected is only slightly bigger than the one being replaced—too big a difference may cause growth to be severely checked. If the larger pot has been used before, it must be scrubbed vigorously. A new clay pot should be soaked overnight in a bowl of water.

Cover the drainage hole with 'crocks' (pieces of broken pot or brick or suitable small stones). Over the crocks spread a thin layer of garden peat, enough to cover them. Then add a shallow layer of the potting compost to which you have added a sprinkle of crushed charcoal.

Take the plant out of its present pot in the manner just described. Remove the old crocks which will be held in by the roots. Gently tease loose some of the outside mat of roots taking care not to damage them—the breaking of a few root hairs may be unavoidable, but it should not exceed this.

Stand the plant in the new pot on top of the compost layer, then gradually fill the space between the soil ball and the pot with fresh potting compost, which should be slightly damp. Most people find that the most efficient way to do this is to take some compost in the hand, align the side of the hand along the top of the pot gradually bringing it towards the vertical and as the soil slips slowly into the pot use the fingers of the other hand to push the soil gently down the sides of the pot. Remember, the compost should contain some charcoal. The quantity is not critical and can be estimated from the amount mentioned on page 39.

Firm down the fresh compost with your thumbs,

rotating the pot as you do so. Add more compost, still firming it down gently, until the level of the stem's base is reached. At this point, tap the pot on the bench a few times to settle the soil; re-potting is then completed.

After re-potting, water the plant carefully and place it in slight shade for about a week. Spray the leaves gently with very fine spray to prevent them from wilting. When the plant is growing normally return it to its usual place.

The most important point of all to remember is that GOOD DRAINAGE IS ESSENTIAL FOR THE SUCCESSFUL CULTIVATION OF IN-DOOR PLANTS.

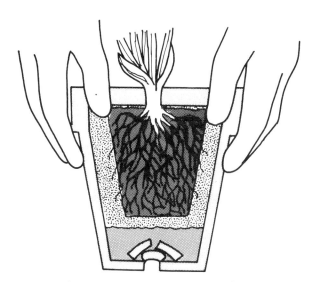

A successfully re-potted plant

What tools do I need?

Very few tools are needed to care for indoor plants and if you haven't the ones listed below, you can often find some substitute among your kitchen tools which will do the job adequately. As you become more deeply interested in indoor plants you will prefer to have the right tools, and they are not expensive.

The bench

The kitchen table will serve perfectly well. With modern soil-less composts, potting is clean and all you will need to do when you have finished is to wipe the table top.

A small trowel

This is one of the most useful tools, although you will often find that some of its jobs can be done just as well with the hands.

Rubber gloves

If you prefer using your hands to a trowel, you may like to keep a pair of household gloves handy.

A tamper

This is a 20 cm (8 ins) length of wooden dowel, 1 cm ($\frac{1}{2}$ in) thick and cut off square at the ends. It is used for pushing down and lightly tamping the new compost into place when re-potting, especially if the gap between the soil ball and the pot is narrow.

A pair of florist's scissors

These have longer handles and shorter blades than household scissors. They are very useful if root trimming is necessary when you are re-potting.

A sprayer

You will not need an elaborate one, but it must be capable of giving a mist spray. An adjustable nozzle is an asset.

A powder puffer

This should be one specially designed to puff a small amount of fine powder on a tiny area of your plant when there is a cut or wound that needs attention.

A thermometer

Choose one of sensible size, say 15 cm (6 ins) preferably with both Centrigrade and Fahrenheit calibrations.

A pocket knife

A slim, two-bladed pocket knife of good quality, which can be sharpened to a fine edge, is the ideal type. The main blade should be 5 cm (2 in) long. Do not buy a bulky 'full of gadgets' knife, they are a nuisance. Nor do you want one with a curved 'pruner' type of blade.

A kitchen fork

This is the most useful tool for breaking up the 'pan' of hard dry compost at the top of a pot when it becomes too dry.

A watering can

Choose one of the modern, plastic type in a size suitable to your plant collection. Remember that you want to be able to water accurately and to avoid marking furniture or carpets while supplying the plants with the correct quantity of water. Do not select a can that is too large, or you will find that it is heavy and cumbersome to handle.

Miscellaneous items

In addition to these basic tools there are some other items which it is useful to have on hand.

Polythene bags of varying sizes

These will preserve humidity, protect plants from draughts and radically reduce the need to water. They are useful when you need to protect a delicate plant after re-potting. If you are going away for a few days, place a polythene bag over your small plants and stand them in a shaded spot.

Liquid fertilizer

A compound, concentrated Biochemical Liquid Fertilizer for feeding indoor plants. 'Baby Bio' is one, there are others.

Powdered fungicide (flowers of sulphur)

You will need this in your powder puffer.

Liquid insecticide

This can be either a contact or systemic type.

Crushed charcoal

$\frac{1}{2}$ kg (1 lb) to mix with compost when re-potting.

Canes

Thin canes of varying sizes to support plants.

Frames

Made of cane or plastic, for use in training climbing plants.

Rings

Fine metal rings for holding stems in position when training them up the canes or frames.

Bass

A soft string which will not cut into soft stems, for tying plants.

By now you will have green fingers!

If you follow all the advice in this section together with that given under the individual plant headings, you can't help but continue to keep your indoor plants alive and well. In fact, you will go even further and keep them both healthy and beautiful. You will feel as proud of your achievement as an artist does when he has completed a painting.

Plant-Think will have become intuitive and you will understand your plants to such a degree that you will know instinctively when the time is right to 'pinch out' so as to improve the shape of a plant or to direct its growth in a different direction.

'Pinching out' is done by pulling the growing tip steadily backwards so that it snaps off at a leaf joint. If the plant is not brittle, then the growing tip must be cut out by pinching it between your thumb nail and your forefinger. Once the growing tip has been removed, both of the tiny buds at the leaf joints will swell and begin to grow, making two stems where before there was only one.

Some plants—Zonal Pelargoniums and Coleus, for example—should be well branched and are consequently greatly improved by this treatment. It should cease when their habit (shape) has been made sufficiently bushy.

Climbing plants require different treatment. With them, you encourage the main stems which you wish to keep, cutting out the weaker side shoots cleanly at the point where they join the main stem. However, a stem may be stopped if you wish the plant to put out two lateral shoots for the purpose

cut back to here

Before

After

cut back to here

of training. Climbing plants will need some support to which they can cling or be tied.

During the winter, a number of climbers, like *Philodendron scandens* and some types of ivy, produce growth on which the leaves are very small and pale. The reason is that the room has been kept at a comfortable temperature for its human occupants, but too warm for the plants. When spring arrives, cut the growth back cleanly to the first good leaf.

Plants like Tradescantia, Zebrina and Ivy Geranium can become very straggly and untidy unless you keep them under control. They should be cleanly cut back to just above a leaf joint. Improvement will then be rapid.

Pruning

Many plants bear their flowers on the new season's growth. Amongst these are Hydrangea, Pelargonium, Fuchsia and *Solanum capsicastrum*. They should be pruned back severely when the flowering period has finished. Cut cleanly across the stem just above a bud, taking great care not to damage it. The remaining stems should average from 10 cm (4 in) to 15 cm (6 in).

Important

Remember to stop feeding and keep the soil only just moist until growth starts again.

Never prune plants which flower on the growth of the previous season or you will be removing all the next season's flowers. *Hoya carnosa* (Wax Flower) is one of this type.

Always cut out dead or diseased stems as soon as they are found. Cuts on thick stems, which tend to bleed, should be dusted with flowers of sulphur immediately after pruning. The sulphur will help dry the wound and discourage fungal infection.

Grouping

In nature, plants rarely grow in isolation and they add to each other's beauty by their association. Bringing indoor plants together in well planned groups will transform their effect in a manner which can be quite breathtaking. A bold, eye-catching display can become the centre of attention. Many small leaved plants, for example, are unimpressive on their own but when combined with larger-leaved varieties provide a striking contrast.

When grouping indoor plants, don't aim for the greatest number of colours or leaf shapes possible. Style and overall form are usually much more rewarding. Perfection in each plant is not essential; a plant which is lopsided and would look unattractive on its own can look excellent when in a group or in a trough.

When planning a group which includes flowering and foliage plants together, be sparing with the flowering plants unless you hope to achieve a really strong, colourful display. If that is the case, then select foliage plants with fairly tall, elegant or feathery foliage to act as a foil for the blooms. Never mix foliage plants and colourful plants in almost equal proportions, or the true beauty of both types will be lost.

The plant tray

This is not the most striking method of grouping plants, but it is one which allows frequent change and greater convenience. The tray should be about 5 cm (2 in) deep and can be made of any waterproof material. A 2½ cm (1 in) layer of small pebbles or shingle should be used to cover the bottom of the tray. Water should be added, but should not reach

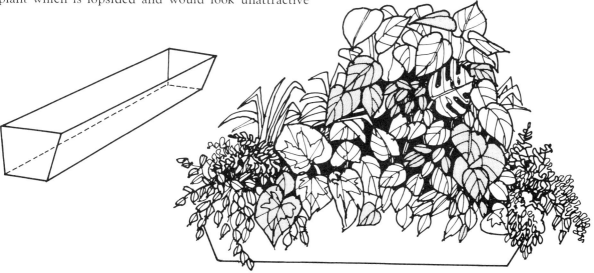

the level of the bottom of the pots which stand on it. The tray will provide the humidity the plants need.

The plant trough

Here you can make a long-lasting garden of indoor plants. Troughs are available in a wide variety of sizes and shapes from garden centres and nurserymen. It is important that the trough should be watertight and large enough to take the pots when they are standing on a thin layer of shingle. There should also be room to pack damp peat around the pots.

It is better to keep the plants in their pots rather than plant them direct into the trough because you can then change them around as you wish. The peat packing must always be kept moist; it provides the necessary humidity and a moisture reserve beneath the pots.

If you water the plants well before you leave on holiday, the plant trough will manage without attention for a period of two to three weeks.

The net

A piece of 2½ cm (1 in) mesh sports netting draped attractively across a portion of wall will provide an excellent support for plants like ivy, in a wall pot fitting.

Plant supports

Support is necessary for many plants and for all climbers.

Hydrangeas have heavy flower heads which, without support, will spread their stems in an unsightly fashion. *Impatiens sultani* (Busy Lizzie) is a vigorous grower with very brittle stems; as they spread they will break off very easily unless supported. Place the supports in the pots before they are needed and loosely tie the stems to them as the necessity arises. Remember that a few untied stems trailing over the side of the pot can enhance the beauty of a climbing plant—but the effect must be planned and not result from neglect.

The wall display

An attractive display of colour and form can be achieved by hanging a foliage plant against a plain pastel-coloured wall. Choose a fitting with a deep saucer and a basically simple shape. Water and humidity are more difficult to provide for a plant that is suspended on the wall so, if it is at all possible, the plant should be taken down from time to time and allowed to 'rest' in a more favourable position, where it can enjoy humidity and perhaps even more light and air.

Indoor plants can make your home sensational

Not so many years ago the standard indoor plant was a dusty, tired Aspidistra in a hideous pot, placed at the window. Modern home design, and the developments in plant culture, and types, have transformed this image. Indeed, many modern homes need the softening and naturalising effect of indoor plants and seem to lack something if they are absent.

There are a few simple rules to follow to ensure that indoor plants make the fullest impact to your decor—

1. Keep your display in scale with the area. *Monstera deliciosa*, for example, can look ungainly and prove obstructive in a tiny hallway, yet it can soften the almost clinical conditions of a large hall incorporating an open plan staircase.

2. Form is often more important than colour, although both have their place.

3. Place the display where it is frequently seen but does not get in the way.

4. Do not display on their own plants which are 'below par'; their defects can be camouflaged by placing them in the company of other plants.

5. In winter, remember that if your room is at a temperature which is comfortable for you, it is probably too warm for most plants. Give some thought to the type of plants you keep in the room and ensure that they are ones which can adapt to the environment. Above all, ensure that they have ample humidity for their needs.

6. Position your plants carefully. Radiators can be a problem but it is possible to buy fittings which fit on top of or above the radiator to deflect the hot air away from the plants.

A redundant fireplace is an ideal spot for plants, providing that the flue has been blocked off and it is draught-free.

In the dining room, wall displays and one striking centrepiece for the table are the most practical. For the table, choose a wide, dwarf arrangement—a big bowl of *Saintpaulia* (African Violets) for example.

The moist, steamy atmosphere of a bathroom can provide excellent conditions for plants which you cannot grow elsewhere. If the bathroom is centrally heated then it is possible to grow delicate varieties in its humid environment.

Holidays

It is distressing to return from your annual holidays and find that your plants have become casualties during your absence. A little forethought and planning can prevent it from happening.

Winter holidays
They do not present severe difficulties, so long as you give the plants protection against frost. Individual plants should be grouped on a table in the centre of a room. Troughs and other mobile displays should be moved away from windows and protected from draughts.

Before you go away, water the plants so that the soil is moist and then surround them with well-dampened peat. Alternatively, place each plant, still in its pot, in a polythene bag of adequate size and close the top with an elastic band.

Summer holidays
Here, there is a real problem. The plants are in vigorous growth and need much more attention. The most satisfactory solution is to persuade a friend who is also an indoor plant enthusiast to act as 'plant-sitter' and tend the plants during your absence.

If this is not possible, place the plants in trays, water them thoroughly and surround them with well moistened peat. Place damp sphagnum moss over the tops of the pots to inhibit evaporation.

Finally, cut off all flowers and flower buds, and cut back slightly plants like *Impatiens* or Geraniums in order to reduce their water demands—such plants are vigorous and will quickly recover on your return.

The method described will not cope with very hot weather, or a prolonged absence. Slipping each plant into a polythene bag of adequate size, with as much as air as possible trapped inside, will also help, of course.

If you are going to be absent for a period of more than three weeks, then one of the automatic watering systems now available will become essential.

Why indoor plants do *not* stay alive and well

The reasons why plants die are legion. The pages on which the plants are described list some of the most likely causes of death or sickness to the plant mentioned. There are nine reasons which account for the bulk of plant failures.

These are:

1. Dry soil

Water is essential to all life. Failures to provide *sufficient* water at *sensible* intervals during the season of the plant's growth will lead to the leaves wilting and the plant's eventual death.

2. Excessive watering

Probably many more indoor plants die from over-watering than any other cause, especially in winter time. The leaves of the over-watered plants flag and it is assumed that lack of water is the reason. A thorough watering is given and the plant succumbs. Both over-watering and under-watering cause leaves to wilt, and it is vital that the two should not be confused. Too much watering tends to cause a yellowing of the leaves which remain soft and pliant. Dryness is more likely to show in the shrivelling of the leaves which become brown, brittle and dry. Over-watered pots often become covered in green slime caused by algal growth. Page 31 deals with over-watering.

3. Strong hot sunshine

Geraniums and a few other plants seem to thrive on strong sunshine. Even so, they are happier if the pot and soil surface are protected from the heat. Many plants will not tolerate such conditions. Always shade the pot and soil surface to prevent baking which will kill the roots.

4. Sharp temperature drop at night

A plant may be hardened to a comparatively low temperature but sharp fluctuations are a different matter. Frost is almost always fatal. Never leave plants on a window sill after drawing the curtains at night in cold weather. A frosted plant may sometimes be rescued by spraying it at once with cold water.

5. Hot dry air

Most artificial home heating dries out the ambient atmosphere. Such dry air is unsuitable to most indoor plants. Provide humidity as advised on page 24.

6. Fumes

Gas and other fumes are most likely to be toxic to plants.

7. Lack of light

Almost all plants need some light and will die without it.

8. Draughts

These are invariably accompanied by sharp temperature changes. Very few plants will tolerate such conditions if they are acute. Even plants which do survive them will not do as well as they would otherwise.

9. Overfeeding

This can result in residues of unwanted chemicals building up in the soil. Eventually the concentrations become unacceptable and often toxic. Underfeeding is a much lesser risk and is usually rectifiable.

Section Two

Introduction

The first part of this book contains general advice on how to keep your indoor plants alive and well. In this section, special care for individual plants is described. Next time you buy a new plant for your home, all you have to do is look it up here and you will find all the basic information gathered together for your convenience. Each plant is treated in exactly the same way so that you know where to look for the information you need. There are five headings.

In addition, each plant has been given a Daisy rating, indicating whether it is ideal for the beginner, or a subject which needs a great deal of care and attention—to be avoided until you have built up confidence in your ability to keep your indoor plants alive and well.

Daisy ratings

 Easy plants which will stand up to quite a lot of mistreatment.

 Also easy to grow; should present no problems provided they are given reasonable consideration.

 These will thrive if the instructions on their care are followed.

There are many more indoor plants than the ones listed here, but these were chosen either because they are easy to grow, or because they offer the most attractive display.

Select from this list and you can achieve almost any type of indoor pot garden or display imaginable. If you delight in flowering plants displayed on their own, there's an excellent selection of these too. There are plants which climb or trail, one which bears berries, and even ferns to act as a foil to more exotic flowering plants when grouped together.

If you've never tried your hand at growing indoor plants, then you are going to find this is a new and fascinating hobby. If you love indoor plants, but never manage to keep them alive and well for very long, this book is a complete and simple guide and once you have developed Plant-Think, you will become more and more adventurous in the range of plants you have in your home.

 Easy to grow.

Asparagus Fern
Balsam
Busy Lizzie
Calathea
Cast Iron Plant
Cineraria
Climbing Fig Leaf Palm
Commelinas
Creeping Moss
Exacum
Flame Nettle
Gynura
Iresine
Ivy Geranium
Ivy
Kangaroo Vine
Leadwort

Easy to grow.

Mind-Your-Own-Business
Mother-in-Law's Tongue
Nerium
Parlour Palm
Partridge Breasted Aloe
Pepper Elder
Polypodium
Sedum
Setcreasea
Slipper Plant
Spider Plant
Umbrella Plant
Winter Cherry.

Geranium
Heather
Hydrangea
Kalanchoe
Lace Leaf Plant
Maidenhair Fern
Maranta
Metal Begonia
Passion Flower
Prayer Plant
Rubber Plant
Shrimp Plant
Star of Bethlehem
Sweetheart Vine
Swiss Cheese Plant
Urn Plant
Zebra Plant.

 A little more care is needed.

Aluminium Plant
Begonia
Begonia Rex
Browallia
Cape Primrose
Christmas Cactus
Cordyline
Creeping Fig
Cyclamen
Easter Cactus
Erica (Heather)
Fuchsia

 Needs a little special attention.

African Violet
Chameleon Plant
Columnea
Dumb Cane
Gloxinia
Indian Azalea
Poinsettia.

Adiantum

MAIDENHAIR FERN

There are many species of Maidenhair Fern and all are dainty, beautiful plants. Good varieties are *cuneatum decorum* and *williamsii*. The foliage of tiny, clear green leaves, often heart-shaped, held on fine delicate stems, and cascading over the sides of the pot, make this fern the perfect foil for other plants.

Temperatures:

Growing season	12–15 °C	(53–60 °F)
Minimum winter	7 °C	(45 °F)

They do not like too high a temperature!

Soil: A soil-less compost.

Where it likes to be: In a light shady position, protected from sunlight. Keep out of draughts and avoid wide temperature changes.

What it likes to drink: Rainwater, to maintain a moist soil condition. Good drainage is essential. The soil must never dry out since this will damage the root hairs. Ferns like very humid atmosphere—see page 24. Spray regularly with a fine syringe in hot weather.

Making it sensational: Feed weekly during the growing season with well-diluted 'Baby Bio' or other plant food (see page 28).

Giving it a rest: There is no marked resting period, and no special routine needed. If re-potting, do not disturb the soil ball. Simply slide it into a slightly larger pot, which is well drained, and top up with new compost, to which a little crushed charcoal should be added in order to keep it sweet. Completely bury the old soil.

When it looks sick:
Wilting fronds: Increase humidity by spraying and by improving environment. Ferns prefer a moist atmosphere in a light shade.
Wilting fronds and yellowing leaves: Stop feeding. If the soil is dry, water generously with soft water but good drainage must exist.
Brown scorched leaflets: Take the plant out of the sunlight which probably caused the complaint. Cut off badly affected fronds close to their bases.

Aechmea fasciata

URN PLANT

A large, very showy Bromeliad with grey-green leaves arranged in the shape of a funnel. It produces a single large flower that looks as if it were made out of pink wood shavings. Each plant flowers only once, then continues as a foliage plant and can easily be propagated from the small plantlets that grow from its base. It needs a potting compost consisting of coarse peat, sphagnum moss, sterilized leaf mould and some grit.

Temperatures:

Growing season	22–24 °C	(72–75 °F)
Minimum winter	15 °C	(60 °C)

Soil: A potting compost consisting of coarse peat, sphagnum moss, sterilized leaf mould and some grit.

Where it likes to be: In a light position but protected from direct sunlight, which will scorch the leaves. Keep away from draughts.

What it likes to drink: Generous quantities of luke-warm water in summer. After the flower has died, a little water can be poured into the funnel of its leaves. It is a dry air plant and does not need humidity. In very hot weather, however, give a mist spray every two weeks or so.

Making it sensational: In the active growth period give well-diluted liquid fertilizer every two weeks. Cut off flower after it fades. Guard against leaf damage which can be caused by direct sunlight.

Giving it a rest: The plant rests after flowering and will not flower again. No special treatment is needed but it does appreciate winter sunlight. The parent plant will probably die. Propagate from the plantlets which will grow at its base.

When it looks sick:
The plant flags: Mist-spray often and ensure high humidity.
The plant leans in its pot: Firm down the soil. Water with soft water in strict moderation. Ensure good drainage or root-rot will swiftly give trouble.
Yellowing or pale-looking leaves: Stop feeding at once.

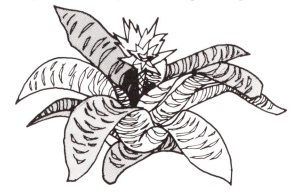

Aloe variegata

PARTRIDGE BREASTED ALOE

Striking rosette-shaped succulent plants with thick spear-shaped leaves. The leaves are broadly striped from side to side with bands of olive green and white and have a narrow white edge. They do not demand a lot of attention.

Temperature:

    Minimum all year   10 °C   (50 °C)

Soil: A soil-less compost mixed with 20% sharp sand.

Where it likes to be: In summer, may be placed out of doors in full sun. In winter, keep in a light frost-free position.

What it likes to drink: Keep soil moist, rather less so in winter. Succulents can survive under-watering to a high degree. Spraying and humidity are unnecessary.

Making it sensational: They need feeding with weak liquid fertilizer only two or three times per season.

Giving it a rest: In winter growth slows; less water is needed. Place in light, frost-free, sheltered position.

When it looks sick:
Browned edges to sections of the leaves: This is usually caused by a combination of mistreatments. Harsh sunlight through glass coupled with gross under-watering may cause it. Widely fluctuating temperatures, coupled with draughts and gross under-watering have an identical effect.
The plant is rocky and loose in the soil: Stop over-watering. Allow the soil to dry out and then water sparingly. The looseness is the result of root-rot weakening the plant's hold in sodden soil.

Aphelandra squarrosa. Var: 'Louisae'

ZEBRA PLANT

A very showy plant. It has wide, pointed leaves of a glossy green strongly veined in cream. It is valued for its striking foliage, but also bears a spike of bright yellow flowers.

Temperatures:

Growing season	18–22 °C	(64–72 °C)
Minimum winter	18 °C	(64 °F)

Soil: A soil-less compost kept moist and springy with <u>soft</u> lime-free water.

Where it likes to be: In a bright window protected from strong sunlight, draughts and wide temperature changes.

What it likes to drink: Lukewarm water. Keep the soil moist and springy to thumb pressure, but never allow it to dry out. Provide humidity; see page 24. Spray daily with a fine mist during dry weather; stop spraying during rest period.

Making it sensational: It can be temperamental. Always follow the seasonal routine, and protect from draughts and fumes. Feed occasionally—about once a month—when flowering. Cut off flower stem when bloom fades. Re-pot in spring if necessary.

Giving it a rest: The plant rests for about six weeks after the flower fades. Reduce watering, stop spraying and feeding until signs of re-growth are seen.

When it looks sick:

Leaves curl and distort: Mist-spray daily and increase humidity.

Leaves drop: Caused by over or under-watering. Water regularly to maintain a good soil condition. Sporadic watering, excessive feeding and temperature fluctuation can also result in leaf loss.

A tall, spindly, ungainly plant: Give the plant more light but not direct sunlight. Pinch out the tips in order to encourage lusty growth.

Asparagus setaceus

ASPARAGUS FERN

An extremely graceful plant with fine feathery foliage which arches from the top of slender, erect stems. It combines superbly with other foliage plants and is undemanding.

Temperatures:

Growing season	18 °C	(64 °F)
Minimum winter	8–10 °C	(46–50 °F)

Soil: A soil-less compost.

Where it likes to be: Is not demanding of light but if too shaded will grow towards the light. Draughts if severe, will cause foliage to lose tiny leaflets.

What it likes to drink: Keep soil well moistened during growing season. Feed with weak liquid fertilizer once monthly.

Making it sensational: This is not a troublesome plant but if it does become unsightly a cut back in the autumn will result in renewed growth from the bottom after the rest period.

Giving it a rest: In winter, reduce water drastically. Place in frost-free position. To re-start in spring, gradually increase watering. As new fronds appear, resume feeding.

When it looks sick:
Browning, dying fronds: Clip out the dying stems and place the plant in a more shaded situation.
The entire plant begins to brown and the leaves begin to drop their tiny leaflets: This is due to over-watering or waterlogging of the soil. Re-pot the plant carefully in fresh soil. The plant will be checked but is likely to recover.

Aspidistra

CAST IRON PLANT, PARLOUR PALM

This is probably the most tolerant plant on earth! It is easy to grow and may well survive fifty years on minimal attention. It is a tidy, symmetrical plant with long pointed leaves which are strong and upright. A variegated form with cream-striped leaves is more decorative but less common.

Temperatures:

Growing season	12–15 °C	(53–60 °F)
Minimum winter	7 °C	(45 °F)

Soil: Mix good friable loam and soil-less compost in equal quantities. Do not over-feed.

Where it likes to be: In a cool, shady position. Sunlight discolours the leaves and may leave their edges an unsightly brown. It is tolerant of draughts and temperature changes.

What it likes to drink: Keep soil fairly moist with lukewarm water. The plant is a heavy drinker so water freely in hot weather. It has no special humidity needs. Spray from time to time to keep foliage clean, gently wiping moisture from the leaves with cotton wool or a tiny sponge.

Making it sensational: The plant can reach considerable size. Re-potting as necessary will ensure continued increase to the preferred height. If the plant becomes too large it can be divided; leaves with roots attached can be potted in compost to form young replacements. Feed every 3–4 weeks with very weak liquid feed.

Giving it a rest: There is no marked resting period. Reduce water by half during colder winter period when plant growth slows down, and continue as above.

When it looks sick:
Brown-edged leaves: Move plant out of sun and check for dryness; the symptom can result from either.
Flagging leaves: Check for waterlogging and if it exists, stop watering until the soil is in a good condition.
Yellowing leaves: Water with rainwater—there may be an excessive build-up of lime in the soil.
Roots appearing on the surface of the soil: The plant is potbound and should be re-potted.

Azalea Indica

INDIAN AZALEA

A beautiful dwarf shrub, usually of good shape with slightly domed top. Very colourful when in flower, since almost the entire plant is covered in blooms, it is available in a number of different shades of red or pink, and also in white, making a brilliant splash of colour. The flowers appear before the foliage matures—the early, pale green leaves enlarge to about $1\frac{1}{2}$ in long, becoming dark green and slightly glossy.

Temperatures:

Growing season	22–24 °C	(72–75 °F)
Minimum winter	12–15 °C	(53–60 °F)

Soil: A soil-less compost with good drainage. The sequestrene it needs is stocked at nurseries and garden centres.

Where it likes to be: Keep in a well lit, airy place, away from direct sunlight. Keep out of draughts.

What it likes to drink: Use rainwater or soft water, never tap water. Maintain moist soil condition; it should never dry out. The plant needs high humidity from the time the buds form right through the flowering period (see page 24). Mist-spray the buds daily with tepid soft water. If they become dry they will drop off.

Making it sensational: Careful watering and cool steady temperatures. Green shoots beside flower buds should be pulled back until they snap off, to avoid sapping the strength of the buds. Feed well-diluted liquid fertilizer weekly. Pinch off dead flowers.

Giving it a rest: The shoots which appear after flowering finishes must be allowed to grow, as next year's flower buds will form at their tips. Re-pot if necessary. Keep the plant, well watered, in a cool room, or a shady spot in the garden from early summer until early autumn.

When it looks sick:
Leaves fall: Place plant in cooler spot.
Leaves become yellow: Tap water may have been used. They are lime-haters and must have soft water.
Buds drop: Place plant in cool spot away from draughts. Mist-spray with tepid water.
Plant looks dull and dry: Water regularly to maintain a moist soil condition. Good drainage is a <u>must</u>.
Pale yellowing leaves: Add a pinch of sequestrene of iron to its next watering.

Begonia lucerna

BEGONIA

An attractive plant with a great number of varieties. The leaves are narrow 'Angel Wings', often red-veined. The flowers, usually coral, though other colours can be obtained, are borne in fine, pendulous trusses.

Temperatures:

Growing season	15–22 °C	(60–72 °F)
Minimum winter	13 °C	(55 °F)

Soil: 70% soil-less compost mixed with 30% peat.

Where it likes to be: Will accept good light or light shade, but needs protection from strong sunlight. It is not very sensitive to draughts or moderate temperature changes.

What it likes to drink: Lukewarm rain water or soft water. Maintain a moist, springy soil condition. Ensure good drainage. Mist-spray plants in hot weather, but avoid allowing droplets to collect on leaves. Provide humidity by a method from page 24.

Making it sensational: Feed weekly with a weak liquid fertilizer. Remove the dead blooms and lower leaves if they become damaged or unsightly. Do not pinch out shoots.

Giving it a rest: Reduce water to maintain moist soil condition and stop feeding. As growth becomes vigorous, increase warmth and provide a little more water. Begin feeding again after one month.

When it looks sick:

Plant flags: Reduce water until soil condition is springy. Check drainage.

Dried brown areas on the leaves: Caused by under-watering or draughts or severe temperature changes. All are simple to rectify and should be done at once.

Buds drop: This is likely from all causes, i.e. over or under-watering, draughts, temperature changes. All must be checked and rectified.

Fungus: May attack open wounds. Dust with fungicidal powder.

Begonia metallica

BEGONIA, METAL BEGONIA

A bushy foliage plant with shiny green leaves. The veins, crimson on the underside of the leaf and black above, produce a unique metallic effect. Compared to some other Begonias, this bears insignificant flowers. Alongside other plants, it provides a striking contrast.

Temperatures:

Growing season	15–22 °C	(60–72 °F)
Minimum winter	10 °C	(50 °F)

Soil: A mixture of 30% peat and 70% soil-less compost.

Where it likes to be: In good light, but away from strong sunlight. It is fairly tolerant, though draughts and wide temperature changes may cause ugly, dried brown areas at leaf edges.

What it likes to drink: Soft, lukewarm water. Maintain a moist soil condition. Mist-spray weekly with tepid water. The plant is not demanding over humidity, but will not like a completely dry atmosphere.

Making it sensational: From March to October feed weekly with diluted fertilizer. In early Spring cut stems to half their length and re-pot. Leading shoots may be pinched out when growth becomes vigorous. Pick off faded flowers.

Giving it a rest: As growth slows, stop feeding and reduce water, still keeping the soil just moist. After re-potting do not feed for six weeks.

When it looks sick: This is identical to Begonia Rex and treatment is the same.

Begonia Rex

BEGONIA

A medium sized, usually well-shaped foliage plant. The large leaves are beautifully coloured with a silver band running parallel to the leaf's edge. They are mostly used to provide contrast with other plants kept in their company.

Temperatures:

Growing season	15–22 °C	(60–72 °F)
Minimum winter	13 °C	(55 °F)

Soil: A mixture of 30% peat and 70% soil-less compost.

Where it likes to be: It thrives in good light or semi-shade, and tolerates draughts and temperature changes. Keep out of strong sunlight.

What it likes to drink: Lukewarm water. Maintain a moist springy soil condition; do not allow the soil to dry out. Mist-spray weekly—droplets must not form on the leaves. This plant likes humidity; use a method from page 24.

Making it sensational: Give well-diluted liquid fertilizer weekly during the growing season. Remove any dead leaves close to the main stem and dust the wound lightly with fungicide powder. Pinch out the flowers as they appear. Only pinch out shoots to produce a good shape.

Giving it a rest: Growth slows in winter. Give less water and stop feeding. Rest for six weeks, then increase light and warmth. As growth starts, increase water to maintain the correct soil condition. Feed when growth becomes vigorous.

When it looks sick:
Plant flags: Stop watering until the soil condition is springy to the touch.
Dry brown areas on leaves: Restore soil condition and water regularly to retain it.
Browning leaf edges: Ensure that the plant is not suffering from draughts or temperature fluctuations.
Fungus: May establish itself on open wounds; use a fungicidal dusting powder.

Beloperone guttata

SHRIMP PLANT

This showy plant is a native of Mexico. It has oval, pointed, soft green leaves. The flowers are hidden amongst distinctive clusters of drooping shrimp pink bracts which overlap closely and appear at the ends of the shoots. The plant may not flower for two or three years, until it is mature, but when it does, the bracts will persist for most of the summer.

Temperatures:

Growing season	15–22 °C	(60–72 °F)
Minimum winter	10 °C	(50 °F)

Soil: A soil-less compost, with good drainage.

Where it likes to be: A good bright position, protected from strong sunlight. It tolerates slight draughts or temperature changes.

What it likes to drink: Maintain a moist, springy soil condition. No spraying or special humidity conditions are necessary.

Making it sensational: The striking shrimp-like bracts last most of the summer; good light improves the colour. Some leaves may drop in winter. Cut back affected stems in early spring when the plant is re-potted and started in growth. Feed weak liquid fertilizer once monthly.

Giving it a rest: The plant rests in winter. Cease feeding, and reduce water. Keep soil just moist. Move to a cooler, frost-free position. In spring, repot, cut back as necessary, increase warmth and light until growth is vigorous. Increase watering, begin to feed.

When it looks sick:
Leaves drop : Reduce watering.
Leaves become limp and dull : Under-watering is the most likely cause.
The plant appears to be drying : The likely cause is root-rot due to waterlogging. It is difficult to rectify and re-potting is a chance worth taking. Then stand the plant in sheltered shade and it may recover.
Curling leaves : Parasite attack. Inspect plant and when found, deal with them as set out on page 35.

Browallia domissa

BROWALLIA

An attractive, decorative pot plant with bright green, heart shaped leaves. It bears a profusion of dainty mauve flowers which will last over a long period if the plant is kept in cool conditions.

Temperatures:

Flowering season   12–18 °C (53–65 °F)

Soil: A well-drained soil-less compost. Plant three to a pot.

Where it likes to be: Keep in a cool light situation, but not in full sunlight.

What it likes to drink: Keep soil moist to thumb pressure. Mist-spray leaves only once weekly. Moderate humidity will be appreciated but is not essential.

Making it sensational: Flowering will continue over a longer period if the site is cool. Feed with well-diluted liquid fertilizer about once a week.

Giving it a rest: The plant should be regarded as 'disposable' once flowering is over, but cuttings will root easily under glass with a little bottom heat.

When it looks sick:

The flowers quickly fade: The plant needs a cooler spot.
The plant becomes lush and blooms sparsely: Reduce or stop feed depending upon the degree of lushness.
Dull sticky-looking leaves: Check for parasite attack. The plants are not particularly prone but it can occur. See page 35 for treatment.

Calathea mackoyana

CALATHEA

An attractive foliage plant. The large oval leaves are matt green, with distinctive brown bars superimposed upon a creamy white ground. It resembles the Prayer Plant (Maranta) but is hardier and somewhat larger.

Temperatures:

Growing season	12–14 °C	(53–57 °F)
Minimum winter	10 °C	(50 °F)

Soil: A soil-less compost.

Where it likes to be: It likes plenty of light. It will tolerate shade but not direct sunlight. It will resent draughts or extreme temperature fluctuation.

What it likes to drink: Keep soil moist and provide humidity. Mist-spray twice weekly and feed with weak liquid fertilizer once a week.

Making it sensational: Cut out unsightly leaves, using a slanted cut, and lightly dust with fungicide powder. The plant is not troublesome. It looks better and is happier in a container with other taller foliage plants.

Giving it a rest: Reduce watering and cease feeding in winter.

When it looks sick:
The plant looks unkempt and dull: Bad drainage or over-watering are suspect and should be corrected. Withhold water for a while. If the soil is waterlogged it may be best to re-pot.
Dry leaves with browning tips or edges: Increase humidity. Mist-spray regularly.
Unsightly leaves with brown edges: See under 'Making it sensational'.
Scale insects: See page 36 for treatment.

Calceolaria

SLIPPER PLANT

A vivid, showy flowering plant and a favourite as a Mother's Day gift. Large pouch-shaped flowers in reds, yellows, and orange are borne in great clusters over broad bright green leaves. The flowers are always speckled and there is both a small and large flowered variety.

Temperature:

Flowering season minimum	8 °C	(46 °F)

Soil: They are not usually re-potted.

Where it likes to be: Likes a good light, cool position but avoid full sunlight. It will droop if placed in a draughty spot.

What it likes to drink: Never allow soil to dry out. The plant likes humidity; without it the leaves may flag. In warm weather, use a fine spray on leaves only.

Making it sensational: These plants are usually bought in flower so feeding is unnecessary. It may be kept and rested in winter but is seldom worth saving. It has been included in this book because the plant is so often given as a gift and rewards the little care that it needs.

Giving it a rest: Treat as an annual and discard after it has finished flowering.

When it looks sick:

Leaves and flowers droop : Probably insufficient water, maintain a moist soil condition. Draughts may affect this plant in a similar way. If the soil condition is good, move the plant to a more sheltered place.
The plant loses its freshness and looks tired : Move it from direct sunlight which is the most probable cause.
Blotchy, unsightly leaves : Check for aphid attack. Too warm a position increases this risk.
Fungus attack can occur : Dust with a fungicidal powder.

Campanula isophylla

STAR OF BETHLEHEM

A pretty flowering plant which can produce hundreds of blooms, especially in its second year. It has an orderly, bushy shape and bears attractive bell-shaped flowers, usually blue, but sometimes white. The leaves are clear green and heart-shaped with serrated edges. It is quite easy to grow.

Temperatures:

Growing season	15–22 °C	(60–72 °F)
Minimum winter	7–8 °C	(45–46 °F)

Soil: A soil-less compost. Use a very weak feed.

Where it likes to be: In good light; not strong sunlight. Avoid draughts and temperature changes; the flowering will be better.

What it likes to drink: Keep the soil in a moist condition. It needs no spraying or special humidity provisions.

Making it sensational: With modest care, this plant can be covered in flowers. Feed weekly when in bud or in flower, with weak liquid fertilizer. Pick off faded blooms to stop seeds forming and weakening the plant. Use a good-sized pot.

Giving it a rest: When flowering stops, cut the plant down to around 4 ins and stand it in a good light, in a cool, frost-free place. Water very sparingly; keep soil just moist. Re-pot in spring and start into growth again in a slightly warmer spot. Step up watering slowly. Re-start feeding as growth becomes strong.

When it looks sick:
The plant looks unkempt and tatty: The likely cause is bright sunshine. Screen it from the sun's rays.
The plant wilts: Correct soil condition to a springy texture; it may have been over or under-watered.
Yellowing leaves: These may result from over-feeding. Have you been too liberal? If not, suspect drainage. This can often be improved without unduly checking the plant. Tap it from the pot, place crocks in the bottom of one slightly larger and replace the plant filling the gap with fresh soil.
Blotchy, sticky-looking leaves: Check for parasite attack. Page 35 gives treatment.

Chlorophytum comosum

SPIDER PLANT

This easy plant has grass-like leaves with a white centre stripe and clear green edges. Small plantlets produced at the ends of long arching stems make it suitable for wall display or hanging baskets.

Temperatures:

Growing season	15–22 °C	(60–72 °F)
Minimum winter	7–10 °C	(45–50 °F)

Soil: A well-drained soil-less compost. However, it is not fussy.

Where it likes to be: A very light position. Direct sun will cause the leaf tips to dry. It resists draughts and temperature changes.

What it likes to drink: Always keep soil moist and springy to thumb pressure. It is thirsty and needs frequent watering if the weather is hot or the plant big. Needs no special humidity treatment or spraying.

Making it sensational: See that it has adequate room to grow, as stems bearing the young plantlets are not supple. The insignificant flowers should not be removed until dead. Feed weekly with diluted liquid fertilizer while growing. Before it becomes too big and coarse, pot up two or three of the plantlets; they root easily and will replace the mother plant once they are growing steadily. No other treatment is necessary.

Giving it a rest: No obvious rest period. Growth slows as light and warmth reduce in winter. Less water will be needed to maintain the soil condition. In winter feed at four-weekly intervals.

When it looks sick:
The leaf tips go brown and dry: This may be over-watering. This must be corrected. It could also be the result of sun scorch. If the soil condition is good, move the plant to a less sunny window.
The leaf tips brown and the plant begins to look unkempt: Re-pot; it has probably outgrown its existing one.

Cissus antarctica

KANGAROO VINE

A useful, fast-growing vine that will quickly cover a wall, room divider or trellis. It is a true climber, supporting itself by tendrils. The long, heart-shaped leaves with toothed edges are a clear shade of green. In shops and offices it can often be seen, the sole survivor in a container once filled with plants. It will fight to live, even in the most unfavourable, dark places.

Temperatures:

Growing season	15–24 °C	(60–75 °F)
Minimum winter	7–10 °C	(45–50 °F)

Soil: A soil-less compost. Keep the leaves free from dust.

Where it likes to be: It tolerates quite a lot of shade but thrives in good light. Do not expose it to hot sun. It can stand wide temperature changes and is fairly tolerant of draughts, but dislikes hot, dry air.

What it likes to drink: In the growing season, it is a copious drinker and will need frequent watering. Mist-spray when the air is dry—daily in summer. At other times, spray and gently wipe leaves when they look dusty. The plant likes humidity. See page 24.

Making it sensational: Give a very weak liquid feed every two to four weeks depending on growth rate. Too much encouragement and it will take over the house. Do not hesitate to cut back.

Giving it a rest: It never appears to rest and no action is necessary.

When it looks sick:
Leaves drop: Improve humidity and cut out unsightly stems once the plant shows signs of recovery.
Leaves crinkle and drop: It is too cold. Place it in an even temperature.
The plant grows lush and invasive: Stop feeding and cut back to a more satisfactory size. Cut at a leaf joint.
Yellowing leaves: Too much light; give it some shade. When bought, this plant may be in too small a pot. Give it four to six weeks to settle before re-potting. Do not over-pot since it will grow very big quite quickly.

Coleus

FLAME NETTLE

These are highly ornamental plants of orderly growth, valued for their foliage. The leaves are shaped like those of the common stinging nettle but are so varied in colours and combinations of colours that two are seldom alike. The flowers are insignificant and should be removed to make the plant stronger. Given a liberal diet and plenty of light, they are among the easiest of all indoor plants to grow and maintain.

Coleus is a good plant to group with others.

Temperatures:

Growing season	22–24 °C	(72–75 °F)
Minimum winter	15 °C	(60 °F)

Soil: A soil-less compost.

Where it likes to be: A south-facing sunny position summer and winter, protected from hot sunshine. It is not susceptible to draughts or temperature changes.

What it likes to drink: Enough tepid water to keep the soil moist, possibly twice daily for large plants. Avoid leaves. No spraying needs.

Making it sensational: Feed once a week (see page 28). Pinch out growing tips to produce a good bushy shape. Remove flowers that appear. Cut off dead or damaged leaves, using a sloping cut, and lightly dust the wound with fungicide powder.

Giving it a rest: It doesn't usually survive its rest period. Coleus is cheap and grows quickly. Buy another.

When it looks sick:
Leaves flag: Caused by over or under-watering. Check soil conditions. Too warm an atmosphere causes leaves to lose moisture faster than the roots can take it up. If the soil condition is correct, this is almost certainly the reason.
Mildew: This may affect open wounds and the treatment is to dust with fungicide powder.
The plant grows spindly: Pinch out the tips to force a lusher growth and stand the plant in better light.
Stained and blotchy leaves: Stop allowing water to get onto the leaves. Check regularly for pests. Mealy bug is a possibility. See page 35.

Columnea microphylla

COLUMNEA

This lovely plant comes from the tropical rain forests of Central America and the area around the Caribbean Sea. It is a trailing plant of tidy habit; long hanging stems with close-set tiny leaves are covered with bright orange or scarlet flowers in season. It is suitable for hanging baskets but is seen to better effect lower down. It is not an easy plant to grow but give it a try; it can be worth it.

Temperatures:

Growing season	20–24 °C	(68–75 °F)
Minimum winter	13 °C	(55 °C)

Soil: It is an epiphyte; in nature it grows in trees, so the soil should be very light: 50% soil-less compost with 50% chopped sphagnum moss.

Where it likes to be: A well lit spot away from bright sunlight. Shelter from draughts and keep warm all year round.

What it likes to drink: Maintain a moist springy soil condition. It must be well drained. Provide humidity; see page 24. Mist-spray frequently, especially in hot weather, once or twice a day if possible.

Making it sensational: Follow the cultural instructions, feed once weekly with weak liquid fertilizer. As buds show colour, stop feeding. Keep soil moist; mist-spray often, more lightly when in bloom to avoid marking flowers.

Giving it a rest: There is no marked resting period. Keeping it a little drier in winter encourages flowering later on.

When it looks sick:
Leaf drop causing the stems to look bare: Ensure that the plant has plenty of humidity and is mist-sprayed frequently. The same symptom can indicate draughts, too low a temperature, over- or underwatering and each of these must be checked.
Parasite attack: Check regularly. If present, use a method from page 35 to deal with them.

Cordyline terminalis

CORDYLINE

The Cordyline is a showy foliage plant. It has long, flat leaves variegated in green and cream with red veins. It cannot be described as an easy plant to keep. It needs some space and is not always suitable for grouping with other plants.

Temperatures:

Growing season	15–22 °C	(60–72 °F)
Minimum winter	10–13 °C	(50–55 °F)

Soil: A soil-less compost.

Where it likes to be: A good light position, not in direct sunlight. It dislikes draughts and temperature changes.

What it likes to drink: Tepid rainwater to maintain a moist springy soil condition; good drainage is important. Always water on the soil. Mist-spray daily and gently sponge the leaves if they appear dusty or dull. The plant likes high humidity—see page 24.

Making it sensational: Feed weekly with weak liquid fertilizer. No stopping or pruning needed but re-pot when the plant becomes cramped.

Giving it a rest: There is no marked rest period. Growth will slow in colder weather. Maintain soil moisture and stop feeding until warmer weather speeds up growth.

When it looks sick:
Plant loses lower leaves: The humidity is insufficient.
The plant flags: This can result from over- or under-watering or poor drainage. Check the soil condition. Ensure good drainage.
The plant pales and tends to flag: Stop feeding. Ensure that it is not subjected to draughts or temperature changes.
Plant looks tired and dull: Mist-spray regularly and sponge the leaves gently.

Cryptanthus acaulis

CHAMELEON PLANT, EARTH STAR

A small Bromeliad with long, very wavy leaves which taper from the centre of the plant to form a low-growing rosette. The foliage is usually mottled or banded with a darker colour. Cryptanthus is quite easy to grow, and very useful in a bottle garden. The flowers are insignificant.

Temperatures:

Growing season	15–22 °C	(60–72 °F)
Minimum winter	10–13 °C	(50–55 °F)

Soil: Add 50% chopped sphagnum moss to soil-less compost.

Where it likes to be: Place it in good light to maintain leaf colour; strong sunlight will shrivel the leaves. Protect from draughts. It withstands moderate temperature changes.

What it likes to drink: Tepid water—cold water could be fatal—poured only on the soil. Keep soil condition moist and springy to thumb pressure. Maintain high humidity as advised on page 24. Spray with tepid water every day in hot weather and once weekly at other times, except during the rest period.

Making it sensational: Pinching out the insignificant flowers to prevent weakening the plant. Give a very weak liquid feed once or twice only per season.

Giving it a rest: It rests after flowering. Water to keep soil just moist; do not allow to dry out completely. Mist-spray once weekly.

When it looks sick:
Plant flags: Check that the soil is moist and springy; if it is, spray to improve humidity. If soil is saturated, then over-watering is the cause. Cease watering until soil state improves and check that drainage is good.
Poor leaf colour: Give the plant a lighter position.
Drying leaves tending to shrivel: This is also caused by inadequate humidity.
Scorched leaf edges: Usually sunscorch. Move to light, shady place.
Parasites: Always check. If found see page 35.

Cyclamen persicum, Cyclamen latifolium

CYCLAMEN

These tuberous plants came from Asia Minor. They have dainty flowers in white, pink, crimson, cerise, salmon or scarlet, carried on slender straight stems. Most are very vividly coloured, even on dull winter days. The heart-shaped leaves are attractively marbled. There are both miniature and larger forms, all capable of surviving several years with proper care. It is better to buy a plant in bud in order to enjoy the display longer.

Temperatures:

Growing season	15–22 °C	(60–72 °F)
Minimum winter	10 °C	(50 °F)

Soil: A soil-less compost.

Where it likes to be: In good light, but not direct sunlight. Although this plant is fairly tolerant, draughts and temperature changes will make it unkempt and unhappy looking.

What it likes to drink: Lukewarm water—cold water could be fatal. Always ensure that the soil is moist and springy to thumb pressure, but not soggy. Do not allow water to remain in the plant saucer. It likes humidity; see page 24. Give an occasional mist-spray in hot weather and shade the plant from sunlight. Do not over-spray; the top of the corm must not be wetted.

Making it sensational: Feeding once or twice per season with very weak liquid fertilizer is ample; never feed when in bud or in flower. Always remove faded flowers to allow other buds to develop.

Giving it a rest: Rest when flowering ends. Reduce watering during this period but keep soil moist and do not allow foliage to die through dryness.

When it looks sick:
The leaf stems droop and lie down: The plant needs watering. Use lukewarm water in several doses to avoid wetting the corm. Recovery is usually swift.
A poor specimen: This may be due to an old, corky tuber and cannot be corrected. Always remove faded flowers to allow the development of more buds.
Sickly plant: Check for parasites—see page 35.

Cyperus alternifolius

UMBRELLA PLANT

No indoor plant is easier to grow than the Umbrella Plant. A good specimen of the variety *C. alternifolius* resembles a graceful group of miniature palm trees and looks elegant on its own or grouped with other plants.

    C. diffusus is lower growing and has broader leaves. It is less delicate in looks than *C. alternifolius* but it, too, is an attractive, useful and tolerant plant.

Temperatures:

Growing season	Anywhere between
Minimum winter	10–25 °C (50–77 °F)

Soil: A soil-less compost, though most open-textured soils will suit it.

Where it likes to be: It will thrive in light or shady conditions. It is tough and not sensitive to draughts or temperature changes.

What it likes to drink: Water copiously. Keep soil almost <u>wet</u>. Leave water in the plant saucer. It is a relative of the Egyptian Papyrus—a swamp plant. Very few plants like their roots permanently in water—this one does.

Making it sensational: Feed it fortnightly with weak liquid fertilizer. Re-pot if necessary because of fast growth. The plant may be divided if it gets too big.

Giving it a rest: No special routine. Growth merely slows in winter.

When it looks sick:
The plant looks tired or the leaf tips go brown: Water copiously. You cannot over-water this plant.
Leaves become unsightly or cause the plant to have a bad shape: Clip off the offending leaves near the crown of the plant. They will be replaced quickly.

Dieffenbachia

DUMB CANE

A striking foliage plant with large elongated oval
leaves which are bright green with blotches and spots
of yellow. The sap is poisonous and if chewed will
cause pain and numbness of the tongue (hence the
name). It should be kept away from children or pets.
It is not easy to grow in living room conditions as
it demands constant warmth and humidity.

Temperatures:

Growing season	15–24 °C	(60–75 °F)
Minimum winter	15 °C	(60 °F)

Soil: A soil-less compost.

Where it likes to be: In the lightest position possible, protected from sun.

What it likes to drink: Tepid water. Ensure that
the soil stays moist. It is a high humidity plant; see
page 24. Mist-spray daily in hot weather, twice
weekly at other times, using tepid water.

Making it sensational: Little feeding necessary;
very weak liquid feed once or twice in the growing
season. Maintain warmth and humidity. As it ages,
the leaves will tend to drop. When this occurs, cut
it back to one-third of its original height. Tend carefully and new shoots will form.

Giving it a rest: No marked resting period—no
special routine.

When it looks sick:
Leaves droop and may drop: You are probably using
too much water which is too cold.
Leaves get dry brown borders: Mist-spray regularly
and increase the humidity. See page 24.
Plant loses colour: It needs better light, though not
full sun.
Leaves droop: Check that soil is moist. If not, water
to correct condition.

Erica X Willmorei

ERICA (Heather)

The winter flowering heathers are often sold as pot plants. The variety recommended is a large-flowered variety and if kept in a cool situation, it will remain in bloom over a long period. Dense spikes of clear pinks florets surmount erect stems and the plant has dark green feathery foliage typical of heather.

Temperatures:

Growing season   14–18 °C   (57–64 °F)

Soil: A good open soil-less compost with a small amount of gravel mixed in.

Where it likes to be: Out of doors until early November. Indoors, the cooler the situation, the longer it will remain in flower.

What it likes to drink: They are lime-haters, so keep soil moist with soft water. Mist-spray once weekly and never allow soil to dry out.

Making it sensational: They are undemanding and need little feeding; once or twice a season with weak liquid fertilizer is enough.

Giving it a rest: Cut back after flowering and place in a cool area until spring. Reduce water in winter but retain moist soil.

When it looks sick:
Dull sickly looking plant: Ensure that only soft water is used. Move plant to a cool place.
Tall plants which tend to open out and become unsightly: After flowering, clip back to a better height.

Euphorbia pulcherrima

POINSETTIA

A handsome plant with large dark green leaves of distinctive shape. The flowers are insignificant but are surrounded by large showy bracts of brilliant scarlet. If the plant is healthy the bracts will last for some weeks. When the bracts finally fade, leaf drop will shortly follow. The plant is not dead, but as it is deciduous it is simply beginning its period of rest. With care it may be re-started in the right season.

Temperatures:

Growing season	15–22 °C	(60–72 °F)
Minimum winter	13 °C	(55 °C)

Soil: A soil-less compost.

Where it likes to be: In light shade in summer; in a bright spot in winter. Draughts or temperature changes cause leaf drop.

What it likes to drink: Keep soil moist and springy to thumb pressure. Tepid soft or rain water is essential as cold water will shock the plant into losing its leaves. It benefits from high humidity—see page 24. Spraying is unnecessary.

Making it sensational: It is not an easy plant to grow; it needs careful watering, good drainage and a fortnightly feed of weak liquid fertilizer, and dislikes gas central heating or fumes of any kind.

Giving it a rest: The rest period begins after the scarlet bracts fall and the leaves drop. Reduce water gradually until the plant is almost dry. Place it in frost-free cupboard until May, providing only enough water to stop the soil becoming dry and hard. In May, remove it from its pot, cut it down to about 4 ins of stem, shake off the old compost and re-pot it with fresh. Place in a warm, bright spot and slowly increase watering as growth re-starts. Pinch out all but two or three new shoots, keeping those which help the shaping of the plant.

When it looks sick:
The plant loses its leaves: This symptom can follow any incorrect handling of the plant. Check for draughts and sharp temperature drops; move accordingly. Check watering; reduce or increase to restore good moist springy soil condition with lukewarm water. Ensure that it has high humidity; see page 24. If the leaves do fall, the plant is not dead. See 'Giving it a rest'.
Parasites: See page 35.

Exacum affine

EXACUM

An attractive small plant often given as a present. Long stems of heart-shaped leaves carry clusters of dainty mauve flowers with vivid yellow centres. It is a member of the Gentian family.

Temperature:
Flowering season 18 °C (64 °F)

Soil: A soil-less compost with 20% good friable loam added.

Where it likes to be: In good light but avoid bright sun.

What it likes to drink: Keep soil moist to thumb pressure.

Making it sensational: The plant is inexpensive and should be purchased early in summer. With reasonable care it will stay in flower over a long period. It is to be regarded as disposable and is seldom worth keeping after October. It can be given easily from seed sown in a propagator in late February or early March.

Giving it a rest: The plant will seldom survive the winter and even when it does, will not be as good as a young plant.

When it looks sick:
Tired, limp leaves: Place plant in a cooler spot. It does not like high temperatures.
Drooping leaves: Check soil condition and water in order to restore a good moist condition.
Browning leaves: Move the plant away from strong sunlight which is scorching it.
Parasites: Spray with insecticide—see page 35.

Fatshedera

CLIMBING FIG LEAF PALM, IVY TREE

A vigorous house plant capable of considerable growth. The variegated varieties require a slightly higher temperature. The species, *lizei*, is probably the most popular.

Temperatures:

Growing season	15 °C	(60 °F)
Minimum winter	4–7 °C	(39–45 °F)

Soil: A soil-less compost.

Where it likes to be: Place in a light non-sunny position. The plant is tolerant of draughts and temperature changes.

What it likes to drink: Lukewarm water. Always maintain a moist soil condition and water on the soil. No spraying is necessary, nor does the plant demand high humidity.

Making it sensational: Feed weekly with weak liquid fertilizer. Cut back in spring for a bushier plant. No pinching out, except for shaping. If it has been in the same pot for a long time and looks tired, re-pot in fresh compost. It will not thrive in too high a temperature.

Giving it a rest: There is no marked resting period.

When it looks sick:
Leaves tend to flag and become pale : Reduce watering, as this is the most likely cause.
Growth too lush and soft : Stop feeding.
Damaged, browning leaves and a tendency to wilt : Reposition out of sunlight.
Aphids : See page 35.

Ficus Elastica var: decora

RUBBER PLANT

Probably one of the best known foliage plants. It grows very erect, with large leaves, and looks well standing alone or in company with other foliage plants.

Temperatures:

Growing season	22–24 °C	(72–75 °F)
Minimum winter	10–13 °C	(50–55 °F)

Soil: A good soil-less compost.

Where it likes to be: In a light position away from sun and draughts. Excessive cold will cause the leaves to fall.

What it likes to drink: Keep soil moist to thumb pressure, with lukewarm water—cold can be fatal; avoid leaves. It is very thirsty and may need daily watering. It needs no spraying but likes some humidity. Feed once a week with a weak liquid fertilizer in its water. Good drainage is essential.

Making it sensational: Sponge leaves to remove dust. Buy special plant polish from the florist to make the leaves shine—it will not harm the plant.

Giving it a rest: No marked rest period and no special routine, but it needs less water and feeding in winter.

When it looks sick:
Leaves begin to drop: This may be due to under- or over-watering. Restore a moist soil condition, with soft, lukewarm water. It may be potbound. Re-pot if necessary.
Leaves drop: It could be the soil condition, draughts or sharp drops in temperature. These should be checked and corrected.
The red stems pale to a dull pink: Stop feeding at once.
Insects: Check regularly for scale insects: see page 36.

Ficus pumila

CREEPING FIG

This is an easily grown climbing or hanging plant much smaller than others of the genus and less demanding of space. Also known as *F. repens*. The plant may be placed in a hanging basket so that it can hang down. It will also look extremely attractive if allowed to climb up through a net hung on a wall. The plant is almost hardy and survives out of doors, in sheltered spots.

Temperatures:

Growing season	12–15 °C	(53–60 °F)
Minimum winter	7 °C	(45 °F)

Soil: A moist soil-less compost.

Where it likes to be: A light position protected from the hottest summer sun. It is reasonably tolerant of draughts or temperature variations.

What it likes to drink: Always keep soil moist and springy to thumb pressure. Water on the soil with tepid water. It likes high humidity—see page 24. In warm weather, mist-spray daily with tepid water.

Making it sensational: Give a weak liquid fertilizer fortnightly. Pinching out is unnecessary except for shaping.

Giving it a rest: There is no marked resting period.

When it looks sick:
Leaves are dry and tend to shrivel: May result from under-watering—restore moisture soil condition. If the soil is moist, check humidity. This plant abhors a dry atmosphere.
Leaves dry and brown: Probably due to too much sunlight. Place plant in another position.
Parasites: Always check. If present—see page 35.

Fittonia

LACE LEAF PLANT

This is an attractive little foliage plant. It has bright green leaves with striking white veins. Variety *F. argyroneura* has deep green leaves with intricate and contrasting silvery white veins which create a lace-like effect.

The variety *F. Verschaffeltii* has red tinted veins and is easier to grow. All varieties produce insignificant flowers.

Temperatures:

Growing season	15–22 °C	(60–72 °F)
Minimum winter	15 °C	(60 °F)

Soil: A soil-less compost. Pot together with other plants.

Where it likes to be: A good light position and allow it sunshine only in winter. It will stand a degree of draught, but likes warmth and dislikes temperature changes.

What it likes to drink: Keep the soil moist and springy with tepid water. Spray daily in warm weather. Provide humidity; page 24.

Making it sensational: Feed weak liquid fertilizer every three weeks. Pinch out flowers to avoid sapping the plant's strength.

Giving it a rest: It rests after flowering. There is no special routine, but it needs less water to maintain the soil condition. A few leaves may drop. Re-growth begins in spring after re-potting.

When it looks sick:
Spotted unsightly leaves: Do not allow water droplets to remain on the leaves.
Leaves look dusty and dry: Spray regularly with a tepid mist spray and ensure that the plant is in humid conditions.
The plant looks well but is not very impressive or is badly shaped: Plant in a larger pot with another contrasting plant. It will enjoy company and both will benefit.

Fuchsia Mrs Popple

FUCHSIA

The plants are available in a great variety of colours, with single or double flowers. Standards (tree-shaped, on a single tall stem) or well-shaped little bushes, they may be trained into pyramids by pinching out in early stages of growth. They will also trail attractively and may be hung from rafters. They are easy, trouble-free plants to grow. The popular Fuchsias all have dainty dark green foliage and a profusion of graceful pendant blooms.

Temperatures:

Growing season	12–15 °C	(53–60 °F)
Minimum winter (frost-free vital)	7 °C	(45 °F)
Rest period (maximum)	10 °C	(50 °F)

Soil: A soil-less compost.

Where it likes to be: In a light, airy position sheltered from strong sun. They are not specially sensitive to draughts or moderate changes in temperature.

What it likes to drink: Water to maintain a moist soil condition. When growing strongly, this is a thirsty plant, but it should not be drowned. There are no spraying or humidity requirements.

Making it sensational: Fuchsias may be trained or grown into many shapes. Feed weekly with weak liquid fertilizer from bud formation to end of flowering. Remove faded blooms to ensure a succession of flowers.

Giving it a rest: When flowering ends, steadily reduce water until the soil is only slightly moist. Place in a cool, frost-free spot for the winter. In spring, give more light and slowly stage back to normal watering and temperature. When the buds begin to swell, cut back the stems, leaving three or four buds on each. As the plant develops, pinch out as necessary to produce required shape.

When it looks sick:
Buds and/or leaves drop: It may be too warm; place it in a cooler spot. Another cause may be over-watering. It needs plenty of water when growing vigorously in warm weather but little and often is the rule.
The leaves droop and the plant has a tired appearance: Probably caused by under-watering. Restore moist soil condition.
Insects: Check regularly. Treat as shown on page 35.

Gynura sarmentosa

GYNURA

An unusual looking plant. The very hairy leaves change from green to purple in colour and it mixes well with other plants. The insignificant florets should be removed at the bud stage as they have an unpleasant smell.

Temperatures:
>Throughout the year   18–20 C   (64–68 F)

Soil: A soil-less compost.

Where it likes to be: For best colour effect, in good light, not in full sun.

What it likes to drink: Keep soil moist to thumb pressure. Slight humidity appreciated but not essential.

Making it sensational: Avoid spotting leaves with water. Cut off unsightly or straggly ones. Cuttings root easily; prepare some regularly to replace the parent plant. Remove flower buds; the flowers smell unpleasantly.

Giving it a rest: Replace plant with cuttings taken about every four months.

When it looks sick:
The purple colouring is poor: Give it more light.
The plant tends to smell badly: Remove flowers and buds; these are the cause. The plant is grown for its coloured foliage only.
Damaged or unsightly leaves: Usually caused by water droplets left on the leaves. Always shake them off.

Hedera helix, Hedera canariensis

IVY

There is a wide variety of ornamental ivies. They are attractive climbing plants with variegated or glossy green leaves. Most are quite hardy and easy to care for, but a few need specialized care. Follow the instructions given on the plant label.

Ivies combine excellently with other foliage plants and are very tolerant of variable light and temperature conditions. *H. canariensis* will achieve magnificent proportions if re-potted when necessary.

Temperatures:

Growing season	16–21 °C	(61–70 °F)
Minimum winter	Frost free	

Soil: A soil-less compost.

Where it likes to be: In a light sun-free position. *H. helix* tolerates some draughts and temperature changes, but the variety *H. canariensis* is more delicate.

What it likes to drink: Tepid water. Keep soil moist and springy—only just moist in winter. Spray weekly in hot weather.

Making it sensational: Feed at two or three week intervals with weak fertilizer. Avoid over-feeding or the plant may become too lush. Ivy hangs, trails and climbs well and is at its best in the company of contrasting foliage plants.

Giving it a rest: No marked rest period; no special routine. Guard against over-watering, especially in cold weather.

When it looks sick:

Dry browned leaves: Can be sunscorch. Move it to a less sunny spot. It could also be under-watering. Check soil condition; keep it moist.

Leaves flag and tend to fall: Almost certainly over-watering. Allow plant to dry out and then water to keep a moist soil condition.

Aphids and scale insects: See page 35.

Where it likes to be: Almost anywhere except direct sun. Shade suits it well. Tolerates draughts and temperature changes.

What it likes to drink: Water, water, water. It is a swamp plant; keep soil moist but well drained.

Making it sensational: You can't, but it provides a fresh green screen in front of or around other plants.

Giving it a rest: It simply slows down a little in colder conditions.

When it looks sick:
It becomes patchy and sick looking: The probable cause is under-watering. Water copiously.
Browning or rotting leaves: Water the soil, not the plant. It likes wet roots and dry leaves.

Helxine solierolii

MIND-YOUR-OWN-BUSINESS

A vivid green little carpeting plant with trailing stems and close-set tiny leaves. It is excellent for screening the pots of other plants, and will grow almost anywhere, but prefers light shaded situations. Do not plant with other indoor plants, but in separate dishes or pots. This plant is a favourite with children—it is dainty, easy to grow and cannot be overwatered.

Temperatures:
Anywhere between   10–15 °C   (50–60 °F)

Soil: Any well drained soil-less compost. It will even grow on moist sandstone.

Hydrangea macrophylla

HYDRANGEA

A most handsome plant with large domed heads of flowers in pink, red or blue. The leaves are deeply veined, heart-shaped and of a rich green colour.

Temperatures:

All year round   5–20 °C   (41–71 °F)

Soil: A soil-less compost.

Where it likes to be: In good light but not full sun. If leaves curl place in a more shaded spot. It objects to draughts.

What it likes to drink: Ensure good drainage and water copiously in growing season. Soil must not dry out. Mist-spray leaves daily.

Making it sensational: Keep in cool place. Support stems if weight of blooms tends to splay the plant. After flowering, cut back a little and plunge pot into soil, out of doors if possible. Bring plant indoors before frost.

Giving it a rest: In winter, reduce watering and keep in cool, frost-free position.

When it looks sick:
Leaves yellow: Plant likes plenty of water, but <u>must</u> have good drainage.
Leaves look tired and wilt: Lack of water causes this. Water and give a mist spray. Recovery will be rapid if it is kept out of strong light.
In blue varieties the flowers become mauvish, then pink: Add a good sprinkle of aluminium sulphate to the compost.

Impatiens sultani

BUSY LIZZIE, BALSAM

Vigorous and easy to grow, these free-flowering plants are very popular, and ideal for children to grow. The leaves are light green and attractive, and the prolific flowers may be red, pink, salmon or white. This plant is very tolerant and will accept a wide range of conditions.

Temperatures:

Growing season	15–22 °C	(60–72 °C)
Minimum winter	12–15 °C	(53–60 °F)

Soil: A soil-less compost.

Where it likes to be: In good light protected from strong sunlight.

What it likes to drink: Maintain a moist soil condition; do not let it dry out. In summer it grows rapidly and needs frequent watering. Mist-spray daily during warm weather. If the leaves droop, the humidity must be increased.

Making it sensational: 'Pinch out' when it is young to encourage a good shape and then stop. Remove faded flowers. As it grows, staking is advisable; the stems are brittle and may snap under their own weight. Give a weak liquid fertilizer weekly.

Giving it a rest: In winter, keep in a warm, light place and water sparingly, keeping soil just moist. Feed while flowering continues. These plants become unsightly with age. Discard and propagate new ones. Cuttings made below a leaf joint will root easily, even in water.

When it looks sick:
Leaves yellow and drop: This can result from over-watering or bad drainage. Reduce water and watch to see if the water sinks quickly through the soil. If it does not—re-pot with special attention to drainage.
The plant tends to wilt: It is a vigorous grower and probably needs repotting.
The plant becomes leggy and ungainly: Cut back unsightly stems at a leaf joint. Dust cuts with fungicide powder. Pinch out tips to make it bushy.

Iresine Lindenii

IRESINE

This attractive foliage plant has an erect tidy habit of growth. The pointed heart-shaped leaves are an unusual dull red in colour with darker markings on them. It makes an excellent contrast with other plants.

Temperature:
Minimum winter 10 °C (50 °C)

Soil: A soil-less compost.

Where it likes to be: In a very light position. The plant will endure direct sunlight if accompanied by good ventilation. Slightly susceptible to draughts.

What it likes to drink: Keep soil moist to thumb pressure and mist-spray weekly.

Making it sensational: These plants are undemanding if correctly watered. They thrive in company with other plants but are often short lived. Cuttings root very easily and should be taken regularly to provide a succession.

Giving it a rest: It is better to strike cuttings than to retain old plants.

When it looks sick:
Pale, badly coloured leaves: The plant probably needs more light, but not sunlight through glass.
Leaves drop: Over-watering is the likely reason. Reduce water to maintain a good soil condition.
Leaves curl: May be under-watering; if so restore a good soil condition. If the soil is moist, look for aphids—see page 35.

Kalanchöe blossfeldiana

KALANCHÖE

This attractive succulent plant of South African origin is a Christmas favourite and deservedly so. The growth is compact and erect, and the thick squarish stems are surmounted by large heads consisting of many small florets of a brilliant scarlet. By artificially shortening the days from early October, the plant can be forced into bloom for Christmas. A number of hybrids offer different heights and colours, but *K. blossfeldiana* retains the most popularity.

Temperatures:

Growing season	12–15 °C	(53–60 °F)
Minimum winter	4 °C	(39 °F)

Soil: A well-drained soil-less compost.

Where it likes to be: In a bright, sunny position protected from hot sun. It tolerates some draughts and temperature fluctuations.

What it likes to drink: Keep the soil moist and springy to the touch. The lower the temperature the drier the plant should be kept, but do not allow the soil to dry out completely. No spraying or humidity provision is required.

Making it sensational: Give weak liquid fertilizer once monthly. Keep soil moist and give plenty of light. It can look rather artificial on its own; in company with foliage plants, it can look sensational when in bloom. Remove flower heads as they fade.

Giving it a rest: It rests when flowering is ended. Reduce the water until the soil is almost dry; then cut plant back to half its height. Give a little water if the leaves tend to wrinkle. In May, gently stage up watering as growth increases, later feed cautiously.

When it looks sick:
Leaves show corrugations: The plant is too dry. Water to restore soil condition.
Leaves begin to yellow: Almost certainly over-feeding. Stop at once.
It is floppy in its pot and looks sick: Root-rot due to over-watering or bad drainage. It is doomed but re-potting is worth a try.

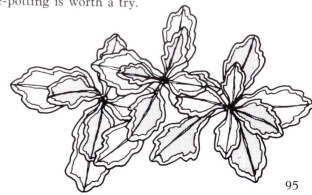

Maranta leuconeura

MARANTA, PRAYER PLANT

These compact plants have large oval leaves and are grown for their ornamental foliage. *Var : kerchoreana* has midgreen smooth leaves with about ten purple markings on the upper surface which give it the common name Rabbit's Tracks. (Underneath, the leaves are a muted purple in colour.) Another variety, *erythrophylla* has bright red veins on leaves which are bright green along the central rib. The common name, Prayer Plant, is derived from the leaves' habit of folding up together at night.

Temperatures:

Growing season	15–22 °C	(60–72 °F)
Minimum winter	7–10 °C	(45–50 °F)

Soil: A well-drained soil-less compost.

Where it likes to be: In light shade and out of direct sunlight. It is moderately tolerant but draughts or excessive temperature fluctuations can result in unsightly leaf damage.

What it likes to drink: Maintain a moist soil condition with lukewarm soft water. It likes high humidity; see page 24. Mist-spray daily in hot weather; weekly at other times.

Making it sensational: Maintain humidity and spray daily in hot weather. Cut off damaged leaves with brown tips. Give a well-diluted liquid fertilizer weekly in spring, summer and autumn, but not in winter. Re-pot into a shallow pot in spring using fresh compost and ensure good drainage.

Giving it a rest: Maintain a moist soil condition in winter. No special routine; the rest period is only a slowing of growth in cold weather.

When it looks sick:
Plant seems loose in the soil and looks tired and sick : Root-rot caused by over-watering. Try re-potting; the plant may not survive but will die if left.
Leaves drying and going brown and dry : Probably under-watered; use soft, lukewarm water to restore soil condition.
Browning tips and edges to leaves : Check the humidity as this is the probable cause. Spray regularly in warm weather.

Monstera deliciosa

SWISS CHEESE PLANT

An evergreen which can be grown to a considerable size, it forms an impressive, long-lived plant. The large, shiny leaves are deeply incised. It produces aerial roots and should be trained against supports covered in damp moss, to which the roots can cling.

Temperatures:

Growing season	22–24 °C	(72–75 °F)
Minimum winter	10 °C	(50 °F)

Soil: A sterile soil-less compost.

Where it likes to be: It requires a light sunless position, chosen with care; it grows to suit its site and may not shift easily. It is wise to avoid draughts and temperature changes.

What it likes to drink: The soil must always be moist and springy to the touch. It is a big drinker and needs tepid, soft water and daily spraying in hot weather. Provide humidity; see page 24.

Making it sensational: Dry soil or air causes leaf edges to brown. Give well-diluted liquid fertilizer once weekly. It will grow quite large, and a stake or moss pole should be provided for its support. Sponge leaves gently to remove dust, or polish them with one of the special emulsions for that purpose. Re-pot the plant when it becomes totally pot-bound.

Giving it a rest: No marked rest period but growth slows in colder weather. Feeding should be stopped and water reduced to maintain soil condition. Spray with lukewarm water every two or three days at this time.

When it looks sick:
Damaged and tired looking leaves : Too dry an atmosphere or draughts may cause this. Improve humidity; see page 24. Ensure that its position is draught-free.
Leaves drying and becoming brown : The cause is likely to be under-watering. Do not drown it. but restore a moist springy soil condition.
Attack by scale insects : Deal with as shown on page 35.

Nerium oleander

NERIUM

A common garden shrub in the tropics, the romantic-sounding Oleander makes an impressive pot plant. Clusters of flowers, usually bright pink, appear at the ends of stems. The long spear-like leaves are normally a clear green but on some varieties they may be a greyish-green.

Temperatures:

Growing season	10–20 °C	(50–70 °F)
Minimum winter	2 °C	(36 °F)

Soil: A firmly-pressed soil-less compost containing a little bone meal.

Where it likes to be: A sheltered sunny position out of doors in summer. A light, airy frost-free spot in winter. It will resent temperature fluctuations if extreme.

What it likes to drink: Water with lukewarm (never cold) water. Keep soil condition springy to thumb pressure. Feed weekly with weak liquid fertilizer.

Making it sensational: Keep in good light in a cool position. Cut off faded flowers.

Giving it a rest: Reduce water considerably in winter. Re-pot in spring adding a little bone meal to the compost. Increase water as growth begins.

When it looks sick:
Browning leaves: Usually indicates bad drainage and a tendency to become waterlogged. Carefully re-pot the plant. Provide really good drainage and avoid over-watering.
The plant does not bloom freely: Over-feeding may result in lush leaf growth. Failure to remove dead blossoms will discourage continued flowering.

Passiflora caerulea

PASSION FLOWER

An impressive climber with unusual and interesting flowers. Blue and white flowers are most common but there is a red-flowered variety. The leaves are smooth and clear green in colour; they usually consist of five pointed fingers, splayed.

Temperature:
Minimum winter   5 °C   (41 °F)
In summer it may be stood out of doors

Soil: A soil-less compost.

Where it likes to be: In plenty of light; it stands full sun. Indoors it dislikes a dark, draughty spot.

What it likes to drink: Plenty of water in a well drained soil. Spraying is not necessary and there are no humidity requirements.

Making it sensational: Don't allow the temperature to drop below 5 °C (41 °F) in winter or next season's flowers will be affected. Feed with very weak liquid fertilizer weekly in the growing season.

Giving it a rest: The plant rests in winter. Reduce watering, keeping soil only just moist until buds begin to swell, then slowly increase water. Feed when growing well.

When it looks sick:
A dull, drab and budless condition: It almost certainly needs more light. It may also be in a draught. Both conditions must be rectified.
Yellowing leaves: Indicates over-feeding which should be stopped. Water with soft water.
Drooping leaves: Check soil condition. It will probably be dry. If it is not then drainage is suspect and the plant may need re-potting.
Aphids: See page 35.

Pelargonium peltatum

IVY GERANIUM

An attractive, useful and easy to grow plant of great value for hanging baskets, balconies etc. The leaves are a clear, bright green, smooth and almost ivy-shaped. These Pelargoniums are really rugged and seem capable of overcoming any conditions except frost. The flowers are similar to those of Zonal Pelargonium but heads are usually smaller.

Temperatures:

Growing season	6–20 °C	(43–68 °F)
Minimum winter	Frost-free	

Soil: A mixture of 75% soil-less compost and 25% good friable loam.

Where it likes to be: In a bright position. It can stand even strong sun and tolerates draughts and temperature changes.

What it likes to drink: Tap water to keep soil moist—do not over-water. No spraying or humidity needed.

Making it sensational: Feed once fortnightly with well-diluted liquid fertilizer. Pinching out is not necessary, but may be employed to train the plant into the required shape. Remove faded flowers and stems.

Giving it a rest: In autumn reduce water until soil is almost dry. Put it in a cool, frost-free spot. In spring, cut back and re-pot in fresh compost with a teaspoonful of bone meal. Gradually return to normal routine as growth begins.

When it looks sick:
Yellow leaves: Usually caused by over-watering. Put in airy place to dry out. Remove badly affected leaves from the main stem by snapping them firmly downwards. Check for root rot. In extreme cases, re-pot.
Black areas on stems: Symptomatic of rot. Cut out affected stems and dust the wound with fungicidal powder.
Other symptoms: See *P. regale* and *P. zonale*, closely related plants.

Pelargonium zonale, Pelargonium regale

GERANIUM

Zonal Pelargoniums are the 'Geraniums' which are deservedly popular for use indoors and out. They have round leaves with scalloped edges and horse-shoe shaped markings. They blossom prolifically in a great range of shades from white through scarlet. The colours are brilliant.

Regal Pelargoniums have large petals, but flower less freely once the first generous flush is over. They make well shaped plants and their range of fine colours and combinations is immense. They are true indoor plants.

Temperatures:

Growing season	12 °C (53 °F) upwards	
Minimum winter (Frost-free)	4 °C	(39 °F)

Soil: Add 25% good friable garden loam to soil-less compost. They prefer a porous calcareous compost which must be well-drained.

Where it likes to be: In a bright sunny spot, with good ventilation, the Zonal Geranium can stand draughts and temperature fluctuations if it must. The Regal Pelargonium likes warmth and shelter, is less tolerant and more sensitive to strong sun.

What it likes to drink: Tepid tap water. Spraying and special humidity are unnecessary.

Making it sensational: Maintain moist soil condition, springy to the thumb. They can stand a period of dryness but will be seriously harmed if over-watered. Feed fortnightly with well-diluted liquid fertilizer. When re-potting add a teaspoonful of bone meal to the compost. Pinch out to induce a good bushy shape; stop removing shoots once they are well branched. Regals require less pinching. Remove faded blooms.

Giving it a rest. Most people start new plants from cuttings. To over-winter, reduce water until the soil is almost dry. Stand plants in cool, airy frost-free place. In spring, cut back, re-pot. Slowly stage up watering as growth increases and give plenty of light and ventilation. Pinch out for shape.

When it looks sick:
Lush, leafy growth but few blooms: Over-feeding causes this. Stop feeding and, in the case of Zonals, pinch out the tips to encourage branching and bud formation.
Aphids: Spray as shown on page 35.
Other symptoms: See *P. peltata*, a closely related plant.

Peperomia caperata

PEPPER ELDER

A very dainty little plant with deeply crinkled leaves and erect catkin-like cream flowers. The leaves are a very deep green, and the plant has a domed compact shape. There are a number of different varieties of Peperomia and all make charming house plants which mix well with other foliage plants.

Peperomia Sandersii has cupped oval pointed leaves which are a bluish-green striped with silver.

Peperomia ornata has deeply corrugated leaves with red veins.

Temperatures:

Growing season	15–22 °C	(60–72 °F)
Minimum winter	7 °C	(45 °C)

Soil: A well-drained soil-less compost.

Where it likes to be: In a light position out of sunlight. It will stand a good deal of shade.

What it likes to drink: Lukewarm rainwater applied under the leaves to keep the soil springy to thumb pressure. It <u>does not</u> like to be immersed in water. Spray daily in very hot summer weather, once weekly at other times; in winter only occasionally on milder days. It likes humidity; see page 24.

Making it sensational: Plant in a shallow dish. If it is in a group, provide a pocket of broken crocks under it. Feed a very weak liquid fertilizer weekly. Cut off damaged or broken leaves and stems and dead flowers as low as possible. Always use a sloping cut to avoid water retention which encourages rot.

Giving it a rest: No marked rest period. Re-pot in spring if it is cramped.

When it looks sick:

The stems flag, letting the leaves droop: Caused by under-watering or too dry an atmosphere. Water the plant, mist-spray it and improve the humidity.

Poor colour variegation: This improves if you give the plant more light but not full sun.

Insect pests: Identify from page 35 and treat as instructed.

Philodendron scandens

SWEETHEART VINE

A prolific climber when conditions are right. Usually it has dark green, glossy, heart-shaped leaves, but other variations are available. The plants are evergreen and are best trained up moss-covered supports as they produce aerial roots. They usually live quite happily in a living room and are seen at their best when mixed with other foliage plants.

Temperatures:

Growing season	15–22 °C	(60–72 °F)
Minimum winter	13 °C	(55 °F)

Soil: A well-drained soil-less compost.

Where it likes to be: It can manage on minimal light, but some sunlight is beneficial in winter. Always protect from hot summer sun.

What it likes to drink: Soft or rainwater to keep the soil moist and springy to thumb pressure. Avoid water on leaves. It is a high humidity plant—see page 24. Spray daily in hot dry weather, weekly at other times but <u>never</u> in cold weather.

Making it sensational: Being a fast growing climber, it needs something to climb on like string or trellis; but cane rods wrapped in moss for the aerial roots to grip are much better and look more attractive. To restrain growth, pinch off top shoots, forcing it to branch. Plants are often sold underpotted, so a transfer to a larger pot and richer compost will be beneficial. After re-potting, maintain soil moisture with just tepid water for a couple of months, then give well-diluted liquid fertilizer weekly.

Giving it a rest: No marked rest period; no special routine.

When it looks sick:
Flagging and curling leaves and weak, soft stems: Check soil condition and if dry, water the plant. The same condition may result from over-watering or over-feeding. In each case cease to do either, resuming watering only when the soil condition has been corrected.
The same symptom may occur even though the watering has been corrected and the plant not overfed: This indicates that it needs re-potting in a larger pot.
A tired, dusty appearance: Insufficient spraying. Increase this and the plant will respond.

Phlebodium aureum

Incorrectly known as POLYPODIUM

A fine strong house plant, this fern is less capricious than most. Long strap-like green leaves wave and curl attractively and are covered with a beautiful blue bloom.

Temperatures:

All year	10–21 °C (50–70 °F)

Soil: A well-drained, moist soil-less compost.

Where it likes to be: Will tolerate shade but grows better in good light. No direct sunlight.

What it likes to drink: Water freely when in growth but ensure that drainage is good. Mist-spray weekly. It requires some humidity.

Making it sensational: As indicated, good light, good drainage and humidity will ensure a handsome plant.

Giving it a rest: It may cease to grow for a time; this is the time to rest the plant. Stop watering and recommence when plant puts out new shoots. As growth increases feed with well-diluted liquid fertilizer fortnightly.

When it looks sick:
The plant looks dry, brittle and tired: You must check all of the following. Drainage must be excellent and the soil moist but not waterlogged. If the plant has dried out, water it and clip off unsightly, damaged leaves. Spray regularly; cater for a reasonable degree of humidity, see page 24. Give it plenty of light but not direct sunlight.

In these conditions, the plant will soon recover.

Pilea Cadieri

ALUMINIUM PLANT

A quickly growing plant, with decorative leaves distinctively marked in silver, it mixes well with other foliage plants and is a suitable subject for planting in an indoor garden or trough. It is also called Artillery Plant because it ejects pollen when a plant in flower is sprayed.

Temperatures:

Growing season	22–24 °C	(72–75 °F)
Minimum winter	10–13 °C	(50–55 °F)

Soil: A soil-less compost.

Where it likes to be: In good light or in semi-shaded conditions, protected from summer sun, draughts and, above all, gas fumes.

What it likes to drink: In summer, water to maintain a moist soil condition. In winter, it should be less springy to thumb pressure, though particles adhere. Avoid splashing the leaves; water stains them. It likes high humidity; see page 24.

Making it sensational: Give weak liquid feed weekly while growing. Pinch out growing tips to force it to branch and produce a good bushy shape. If you do not, the plant grows leggy and ungainly.

Giving it a rest: It rests in winter. As growth ceases, reduce water and stop feeding. Re-pot in spring. Cut back stems to half their height and maintain a moist soil condition. Six weeks after re-growth begins, resume feeding.

When it looks sick:
Poor colouring: This results from insufficient light. Improve the light but do not place the plant in direct sunlight.
Dry, dusty-looking leaves, lacking a healthy sheen: Inadequate humidity will cause this. Improve the humidity and mist-spray regularly.
Stained blotchy leaves: Caused by water splashes. Always shake them off.
Poor growth and yellowing foliage: Water the plant with $\frac{1}{4}$ oz magnesium sulphate (Epsom Salts) to 1 pint of water—30 gm to 1 litre.

Plumbago auriculata

LEADWORT

The pretty little flowers of the leadwort will last for months on end. The leaves are oval and a rich green colour. Long shoots may need some support. The plant is excellent for use in tubs.

Temperatures:

Growing season	10–21 °C	(50–70 °F)
Minimum winter	4 °C	(39 °F)

Soil: A soil-less compost.

Where it likes to be: In summer the plant can be stood out of doors. In winter a light, frost-free, cool spot will suit it.

What it likes to drink: Keep soil moist. There are no humidity requirements.

Making it sensational: The plant will flower for some months on end. Feed with very diluted liquid weekly. Remove faded blooms.

Giving it a rest: In late September, transfer the plant to a cool, well-lit winter position. Reduce watering to keep soil just moist. The site must be frost-free. In spring, re-pot and as growth starts slowly increase water.

When it looks sick:

Yellowish foliage which looks dull and anaemic: Almost certainly the result of root damage caused by over-watering. Allow the soil to dry and reduce the amount of water given.

Excessive leaf production and fewer flowers: Over-feeding. Be sparing with feed.

Saintpaulia ionantha

AFRICAN VIOLET

A low-growing plant with dark green, hairy leaves growing in a circle around its centre. Clusters of vivid flowers occupy the centre of the plant when it is in bloom. It will flower for several months given reasonable care. There are varieties in white, red, purple or pink and others with double blossoms. The most popularly sold are of the single purple variety.

Temperatures:

Growing season	15–22 °C	(60–72 °F)
Minimum winter	13 °C	(50 °F)

Soil: A moist soil-less compost.

Where it likes to be: In a light position out of full sun, except in winter when some sunlight is appreciated. They dislike draughts and sudden temperature changes.

What it likes to drink: Use tepid soft water introduced below the leaves, straight onto the soil. Do not splash; droplets mark the leaves and cause holes. Water must not get into the crown of the plant; it remains and causes rotting. The plant needs high humidity; see page 24. Mist spray daily in hot weather, weekly at other times.

Making it sensational: Snip off faded flowers and damaged leaves. Avoid sun damage. Re-pot it when necessary; too large a pot results in lush soft growth and fewer flowers. Give very weak liquid fertilizer fortnightly.

Giving it a rest: After flowering, it takes a short rest but this is more beneficial if extended by reducing water gradually until the soil is kept just moist for six weeks. Annual re-potting is essential in a wide shallow pot so that the leaves rest on its rim. Then gradually increase watering and in summer feed the plant.

When it looks sick:
Spotted, unsightly leaves: Caused by water droplets remaining on the leaves. Always shake them off.
The plant looks dull and dry: Check that soil condition is correct. If it is, move the plant to an East-facing window away from bright sunlight. Mist-spray regularly.
Mealy bugs: If found—see page 37.

Sansevieria trifasciata

MOTHER-IN-LAW'S TONGUE

A tall, spiky plant which looks like a cactus or succulent, but is actually of the Lily family. The thick spear-like leaves can reach a considerable height and are very erect. They are variegated, pale and darker green. *Var. laurentii* also includes cream in its patterning. The flowers are insignificant.

Temperatures:
Growing season   16–21 °C   (61–70 °F)
Temperature should be constant throughout the year. The plant cannot stand wide temperature changes.

Soil: A soil-less compost, with 10% added sand.

Where it likes to be: In a light position out of direct sunlight, away from draughts and temperature changes.

What it likes to drink: Lukewarm water to keep the soil just moist. Excessive water in winter is disastrous; the leaves rot at soil level and the plant dies. No spraying or humidity needed.

Making it sensational: If it tries to flower, pinch out the flowering stem, as it weakens the plant. Give a very dilute liquid fertilizer once monthly. Never risk over watering—in winter it needs only just enough to stop total drying out. Do not over-pot. Re-pot only when the plant forces it way out. Maintain an even temperature.

Giving it a rest: There is no clearly defined rest period.

When it looks sick:
Brown, striated areas along the leaf edges: Scorch by strong sunlight. They may also be due to under-watering. Keep it in light shade; water if the soil is dry.
    The commonest cause of death has no symptom. Over-watering causes the leaves to rot below the soil surface. Never, never over-water this plant.

Sedum seiboldii

SEDUM

One of a numerous species. Small pink flowers on the ends of trailing stems decorated with thick rounded leaves which are cream centered with sage green edges. May be grown on a balcony in summer.

Temperatures:
Minimum winter   5–10 °C   (41–50 °F)

Soil: Mix 20% horticultural sand with soil-less compost. Ensure good drainage.

Where it likes to be:
In a sunny position shaded or protected from hot sun through glass.

What it likes to drink: Keep soil moist. No special humidity or spraying requirements.

Making it sensational: Cut off faded flowers or stems that become bare or straggly. The plant is an excellent trailer and blends well when planted in front of other subjects. Feed with weak liquid fertilizer monthly.

Giving it a rest: Keep dry in winter at a temperature of 5–10 °C (41–50 °F). In spring, re-start watering and feeding. Re-pot if necessary.

When it looks sick:
The fleshy leaves begin to take on a yellow tinge and drop easily: This is a symptom of root damage caused by excessive watering or excessive feeding. In either case reduce the amount given. If the soil is saturated, re-potting will give the plant a check but will probably save it.

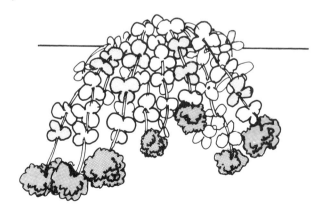

Selaginella

CREEPING MOSS

There are several species of Selaginella. They often resemble mosses but are really tiny ferns. Others look like miniature trees sometimes with white and green variegated foliage. They are all very attractive and combine well with the other plants. Suitable for bottle gardens.

Temperatures:

Growing season	12–20 °C	(53–58 °F)
Minimum winter	12 °C	(53 °F)

Soil: Soil-less compost in shallow dishes with adequate drainage.

Where it likes to be: In a well shaded site away from draughts and extreme temperature changes. Strong light damages the fronds.

What it likes to drink: Keep well watered in shallow pots. Pay special attention to drainage, humidity and regular mist-spraying are essential. It likes a moist root run but dislikes waterlogged soil.

Making it sensational: Feed two or three times each season with very weak liquid fertiliser. Maintain regular watering and humidity.

Giving it a rest: Reduce water slightly in winter; protect from draughts and sharp temperature changes.

When it looks sick:
The tips of the leaves turn brown and dry : The condition progresses down the plant. As parts of the plant die off, it becomes unsightly and open. Over-feeding, over-watering, under-watering, poor humidity and poor drainage can all have this effect. All must be checked and corrected.

Senecio

CINERARIA

Still widely known, incorrectly, as Cineraria. It is a large-leaved plant with brilliant daisy-like flowers borne in dense heads during winter and spring. The colours cover a very wide range; blue with white centres are the most commonly seen.

Temperature:
Minimum, growing season   12 °C   (53 °F)

Soil: A soil-less compost.

Where it likes to be: A cool light position out of full sun. It objects to draughts which make leaves go limp.

What it likes to drink: Keep soil moist—never let it dry out. It likes some humidity and in dry weather, mist-spray the leaves. This prevents excessive respiration and stops leaves from wilting.

Making it sensational: They are usually bought in flower and feeding is unnecessary. If kept in cool conditions they last very well.

Giving it a rest: They can be over-wintered but are not worth the trouble as they are quite cheap and second year plants seldom equal new young specimens.

When it looks sick:
Flagging leaves hanging limply over the sides of the pot: Check soil condition; if dry, water. Give the leaves a fine spray. If the soil is moist, spray only and move into light shade to recover.
Erect, lack-lustre leaves probably with a blotchy appearance: Possibly aphids—see page 35.
The mildewy growth of fungus: Dust promptly with a fungicidal powder.

Setcreasea purpurea

SETCREASEA

A horizontally-growing plant. There is a fine purple-blue bloom on the spear-shaped leaves. It is related to the Tradescantia which it resembles. It trails well and is suitable for combining with other plants.

Temperature:

Minimum all year   5 °C   (41 °F)

Soil: A soil-less compost with 20% good friable loam added.

Where it likes to be: It accepts shade but good light produces better colouring. It tolerates draughts and temperature changes.

What it likes to drink: Keep soil well moistened. Mist-spray once weekly. Do not spot the leaves.

Making it sensational: Feed monthly with very weak liquid fertilizer. Remove dried leaves, pinch out tips if stems become denuded or too leggy. It can be cut back if it becomes untidy or to encourage denser growth.

Giving it a rest: Reduce water and stop feeding in winter. Slowly return to normal routine as warmer weather and increased light stimulate new growth.

When it looks sick:

Blotchy, unsightly leaves: Caused by allowing water droplets to remain on the leaves.

Poor colouring, leggy stems, dry, dead leaves: All of these result from inadequate light. Move it to a brighter spot. Trim off unsightly stems and dead leaves, pinch out tips and the plant should soon improve.

Root-rot: Caused by over-watering or poor drainage. Carefully re-pot and reduce the amount of water given.

Sinningia Hybrids

GLOXINIA

One of the most beautiful and sensational of house-plants. Clusters of large, velvety, trumpet-shaped flowers surmount beautiful foliage in this low growing plant. A vast range of very pure colours is available.

Temperatures:

Growing season	22–24 °C	(72–75 °F)
Minimum winter	Store tubers in dry frost-free place.	

Soil: A soil-less compost.

Where it likes to be: In plenty of light but protected from sun and draughts.

What it likes to drink: Lukewarm water daily to keep soil moist in growing period. Avoid water on leaves or flowers. Mist-spray daily in hot weather when not in flower. Avoid droplets on leaves—shake them off. It likes humidity—see page 24.

Making it sensational: Give weak liquid fertilizer once every week. Carefully cut off faded blooms and damaged leaves; dust any open wounds lightly with a powder fungicide.

Giving it a rest: After flowering, stop water and feeding; let it die down completely. Dust with fungicide powder and place in dark, frost-free spot until spring. In late April, re-pot the tubers in fresh compost and in a clean pot. Place in a warm position and water lightly. When growth starts, increase water and begin slowly to feed. Keep water away from the crown of the plant.

When it looks sick:
Leaves limp and dull, the flower trumpets tending to collapse: Check the soil; if dry, water and spray. If the soil is moist, spray the plant and improve humidity—see page 24.
Leaves firm but lacking a healthy deep green gloss: May be aphids—treat as shown on page 35.
Rotting spots on leaves: Caused by water droplets after watering or spraying. Dust affected areas lightly with fungicidal powder.

Solanum capsicastrum

WINTER CHERRY

An attractive, compact shrub from Brazil. It grows from 1–2 feet high, has neat, dark green leaves and during autumn and winter bears masses of coloured berries. The colour of these varies with the degree of ripeness so that all colours from white to red may be seen on the plant at the same time. The berries are poisonous and must be kept out of the reach of small children.

Temperatures:

Growing season	12–21 °C	(53–70 °F)
Minimum winter	7–10 °C	(45–50 °F)

Soil: A soil-less compost.

Where it likes to be: A light position which permits only a little sunshine. Excessive draughts or temperature changes may cause the berries to drop—and sometimes the leaves.

What it likes to drink: Keep the soil just moist and springy to the touch. No special humidity needs, but mist-spraying when in flower helps to set the berries. Pollination is helped by using small, soft brush on the blooms.

Making it sensational: Feed weak liquid fertilizer once weekly. Keep in a cool spot; avoid over-watering. Keep in one place or berries may fall.

Giving it a rest: It rests after the berries have fallen, usually in early spring. Re-pot, shaking out old compost and replacing with fresh. Place in a cool, bright spot; water to keep a good soil condition. Feed as growth increases. When re-potting, straggly plants can be gently cut back. In summer, it may be put outside in a sheltered spot, but bring it inside by late September. Keep in good light and rotate from time to time.

When it looks sick:

Leaves and/or berries begin to drop: May be due to over-watering; check the soil condition. The cause may also be a sharp temperature rise; put in a cool place.

The leaves become yellow even though the soil condition is good: Magnesium deficiency. Water it with a solution of magnesium sulphate (Epsom Salts) $\frac{1}{4}$ oz to 1 pint. If the shock has been too great it may lose leaves and berries; allow the plant to rest. It will grow again in due season.

Streptocarpus

CAPE PRIMROSE

Streptocarpus hybrids are available in a range of colours from white through pink to mauve. They are pretty plants with long, bright green oval leaves like those of the primula. The dainty flowers are carried in clusters at the tops of slender stems, of which there may be quite a number on a well grown plant.

Temperatures:

Growing season	12–22 °C	(53–70 °F)
Minimum winter	12 °C	(53 °F)

Soil: A soil-less compost. Humidity is necessary.

Where it likes to be: In good light in winter; never in full sun. It dislikes draughts and temperature changes.

What it likes to drink: Keep soil moist to thumb pressure. Never allow to dry out as the leaves will flag badly and may be damaged. Mist-spray regularly, except in winter.

Making it sensational: Give very weak liquid fertilizer weekly in growing season. Stop when plant begins to flower. Remove faded flowers and stems.

Giving it a rest: Reduce water but do not allow foliage to die down. Maintain minimum temperature of 12 °C (53 °F). Re-pot in spring with soil-less compost.

When it looks sick:
Flagging leaves, lacking their usual gloss: Check the soil condition; if dry, water and use a fine spray on the leaves. If the soil is moist, spray only and improve the humidity—see page 24. Keep out of strong sunlight.
Leaves pale and become dull: Aphids—see page 35.
Mildew on damaged leaves: Dust with a fungicidal powder.

Zebrina pendula

COMMELINAS

Zebrina pendula is a very popular plant often mistaken for a Tradescantia which has similar form and growth habit. The variety 'Quadricolor' has green, purple and white-striped leaves, whose crystalline shimmer makes them most attractive. It trails well and is fine kept in a fairly high position. This is one of the least demanding plants. It mixes well with other indoor foliage plants.

Temperatures:

Growing season	12–22 °C	(53–72 °F)
Minimum winter	7–10 °C	(45–50 °F)

Soil: A mixture of soil-less compost and 20% good friable garden loam.

Where it likes to be: In good light which promotes good colour. It tolerates shade, draughts and varying temperatures. Avoid hot sunlight.

What it likes to drink: Tepid water. Maintain a moist soil condition. It needs no regular spraying but mist-spraying occasionally. No special humidity required.

Making it sensational: Give a weak liquid fertilizer monthly. Trim the stems to keep it tidy and attractive.

Giving it a rest: It grows continuously. There is no marked resting period but less water is needed in winter to maintain the correct soil condition.

When it looks sick:
The distance between leaves on the same stem is long: The plant is becoming 'drawn'; give it more light.
Leaves die, becoming brown, dry and brittle: The plant is grossly under-watered. Plunge the plant, as directed on page 22, to wetten the soil ball.
The leaf colour becomes glossy green instead of retaining its purple striping: This is a symptom of inadequate light.

Where it likes to be: It needs plenty of light but should be protected from hot sun. It likes a fairly even temperature.

What it likes to drink: Use lukewarm water to keep the soil just moist to thumb pressure until the buds form; then increase the amount slightly as the buds swell, avoiding the leaves. Excessive watering causes buds to drop. Never spray.

Making it sensational: Feed very occasionally with liquid fertilizer heavily diluted. It must be kept in the same position and never handled or moved. Carefully twist off dead blooms.

Giving it a rest: It rests when flowering is over. Reduce water. After six weeks, re-pot into compost with a little sandy grit added. Do not use too big a pot; this stimulates leaf growth and reduces the flowers.

When it looks sick:
The leaves assume a corrugated appearance: This is the effect of under-watering. Water the plant but avoid over-watering.
The flower buds drop: This happens if the plant is moved or rotated after the buds have formed. Cease feeding at this point.
Pale sickly looking leaves result from over-feeding: Stop feed and water with soft water.
Mealy bugs: Deal with them as shown on page 37.

Zygocactus truncatus,
Shlumbergera Russeliana
CHRISTMAS CACTUS, EASTER CACTUS

These are the easiest to grow of all leafy cacti, and are remarkably floriferous. The leaves form part of a segmented stem. Both these plants come from Brazil. *Zygocactus* is the true Christmas cactus; *Shlumbergera* flowers a month or two later and is known as the Easter cactus. They can be obtained with flowers of delicate shades of white, pink, and flamingo reds and oranges. They are highly useful for providing colour in mid-winter and early spring.

Temperatures:

Growing season	22–24 °C	(72–75 °F)
Minimum winter	10 °C	(50 °F)

Soil: Soil-less compost to which 10% sand has been added.

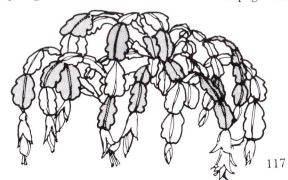

Index